DECISIVE BATTLES

The Turning Points of World War II

WINDWARD

Editor: Len Cacutt   Art Editor: Gordon Robertson
Designer: John Fitzmaurice   Production: Richard Churchill

Published by Windward, an imprint owned by W.H. Smith & Son Limited   Registered No. 237811 England
Trading as WHS Distributors, St John's House, East Street, Leicester LE1 6NE
© Marshall Cavendish Limited 1986

ISBN 0-7112-0453-5
Typeset in Rockwell by Quadraset Limited, Midsomer Norton, Avon
Printed and bound in Spain by Artes Graficas Toledo S.A.
D. L. TO:997-1986

CONTENTS

A tripod-mounted German MG34 on the Aisne. The crossing of that river was to entail some of the severest fighting yet for German infantry in 1940. Gen. A. Schubert of the attacking 23 Corps wrote in his diary that French snipers fought to the last cartridge even when cut off in their tree perches by the German advance on 9-10 June. He was reminded of French heroism at Verdun in 1916. On both the Somme and the Aisne French resistance dislocated German plans of attack for the first 36 hours, until defences up to 19.5 km (12½ miles) deep had been penetrated.

FOREWORD

Any listing of 'decisive' battles of any campaign is bound to be subjective, bound to stimulate argument, if only for the fact that different observers see different aspects of a war and may apply different criteria. Thus an aviation specialist might see the thousand-bomber raid on Cologne as being decisive in the context of demonstrating Bomber Command's capabilities, and thus influencing their subsequent operations, whereas an economic warfare specialist would dismiss the raid as being of no significance in disrupting the German war economy and having no overall effect on World War 2.

The battles which have been selected for this book are equally arguable, but each, in its own way, was to have some greater significance to the progress of the war as a whole. The battle of the River Plate was an isolated naval action in most respects, but it signalled the end of German commerce raiding. The battle for Crete put an end to German parachute operations; henceforth German paratroops were used as ground infantry and opportunities which could have been exploited by airborne attack were ignored.

The gradual post-war revelation of the 'inside stories' of various aspects of the war has given cause to re-assess various battles, and the principal revelation came in the mid-1970s with the gradual release of information on the British decipherment of the German 'Enigma' codes. This led to discussions as to whether Allied commanders should not have done better, since they were fully informed of their enemy's intentions at all times.

Enigma information was not a constant flow, but an intermittent supply which depended upon the code-breakers' ability to master the latest German variations and also upon pure chance as to which message was deciphered first. The decipherers might spend days before coming upon the one which gave the plan of attack; by which time it was stale news.

Moreover there was always the overriding need to conceal the origin of the information; Allied activity on a quiet sector in advance of a German attack would be a certain indication that secrets had leaked, and if this had caused their cipher system to be radically overhauled the strategic loss would have far outweighed the gain on the battlefield.

One fact which post-war analysis has made clear is the value of Herr Hitler to the Allies. Had he left the conduct of warfare to his commanders, who were by and large a highly competent group, the final outcome might very well have been a good deal different. But his determination to have the final word and his paranoid insistence upon never giving ground gained were both contributions to the ultimate German defeat.

The art of warfare, it has been said, is the art of the possible; Hitler preferred the beguilements of the probable, and made his dispositions accordingly.

Had the German High Command been given its head on 6 June 1944 there is every likelihood that the Allied landings in Normandy would have been contained for very much longer than they were. Had Hitler not made his decision to concentrate on 'offensive' weapons rather than 'defensive' weapons the Luftwaffe might have been a totally different force and might have made a significant difference to the D-Day invasion and the Normandy campaign.

But there. Warfare is entirely a matter of 'What if . . .' and the commander who wins is the commander who is more prepared for the unexpected disaster. Read the accounts of the battles which follow, and contemplate what might—just might—have happened had they gone the other way.

1939-40

When war was declared on Germany at 11 o'clock on a bright Sunday morning on 3 September 1939, Britain braced itself for the expected onslaught by air. In fact, the air-raid sirens sounded in London only a short while after the radio (then still called the 'wireless') had informed the nation that it was in a state of war; the population responded by immediately going to the air-raid shelters that had been built in readiness. But the alert was a false alarm, triggered off by an unidentified civilian aircraft detected in the air space over the East Coast.

While Poland suffered as the Panzer columns thrust eastwards throughout September, and Britain's Commonwealth began declaring its own state of war against Hitler's Reich, the US remained uncommitted. It would be the underhand Japanese attack on Pearl Harbor a year later which would act as the catalyst to bring the military and industrial resources of the US alongside those of the Allies.

The air war was fairly low key, with the RAF's bomber forces still equipped with slow, vulnerable machines such as the Bristol Blenheim, unlike the battle-tested He111s and Do17s of the Luftwaffe which had perfected their trade in the skies over Spain in the cause of General Franco's right-wing insurgency.

But it was not long before Britain's merchant shipping was suffering from the predations of Germany's U-boat fleet, the ferociousness of its operations being made abundantly clear when the SS *Athenia* was torpedoed with cruel loss of life.

While Britain fared well in her own blockade to prevent vital supplies reaching Germany, the Royal Navy's superior strength and numerical advantage holding up well, she was not so successful in combatting the growing number of attacks on merchant shipping delivering the essentials an island race needs to conduct major warfare and at the same time feed its population. The first attack on a Britain-bound convoy came on 16 September with the loss of one merchantman. And the next day the aircraft carrier HMS *Courageous* was sent to the bottom by *U29* along with over 500 of her crew.

Then one of Germany's three pocket-battleships was brought into action. The *Graf Spee* was a formidable fighting ship, capable of sinking any Royal Navy unit in the Atlantic at that time. After sinking shipping off the West African coast she moved across the Atlantic to pick off helpless merchantmen by using her big guns at a safe distance.

There were three Royal Navy cruisers in the area at the time, the *Ajax*, *Achilles* and *Exeter*. The group was led by Commodore Harwood in a dashing and brilliant manner.

The first battle in this chapter tells the thrilling story of how, unaided by Naval Intelligence, Harwood tracked *Graf Spee* down, peppered her with the comparatively small armament of the British cruisers and drove her into the mouth of the River Plate. The end of the *Graf Spee* is one of the most dramatic incidents of World War 2. It was a tremendous boost to the morale of those Britons who were beginning to need encouragement. There follows the limited but vital engagement near Arras, where a small British armoured force kidded Rommel into believing he was fighting a very superior group. The outcome enabled the BEF to get away at Dunkirk.

After the BEF's withdrawal, Hitler turned his attention to crushing Central France. The result was never in doubt, but the German army lost far too many soldiers as the result of very determined French resistance.

Last in this chapter is a battle that needs no introduction: the attempt by Hitler to destroy the RAF before invading Britain. In the end he made a disastrous tactical blunder, an error which was to cost Germany the war in Europe.

BATTLE OF THE RIVER PLATE

Commodore Henry H. Harwood, OBE, RN, stabbed a finger on the chart aboard his flagship, the light cruiser HMS *Ajax*: 'That's where she'll turn up next,' he predicted confidently. He thought his quarry was the German pocket-battleship *Admiral Scheer*. He further predicted—though with less skill and some luck—that the enemy ship would arrive astride the rich South American trade routes of the River Plate area on 12 December 1939. He was one day out.

The warship was in fact the *Admiral Graf Spee* and at the time she was 3200 km (2000 miles) away celebrating the sinking of the ninth and last victim of her 12-week cruise as a commerce raider. *Kapitan zur See* Hans Langsdorff and the ship were well-matched but when put to the test of battle it was the man who failed, not the ship. *Graf Spee* sailed from Wilhelmshaven on 21 August 1939, 10 days before the outbreak of war, destination mid-Atlantic. She was accompanied by a supply ship, the notorious *Altmark*, later captured as a prisonship. Action with enemy naval forces was to be avoided at all costs, except to further the primary objective.

Graf Spee's last victory

On 7 December *Graf Spee* sank her last victim, the cargo vessel *Streonshalh*. This sinking brought her total to nine British ships and 50,089 tons. Not a single life had been lost during these sinkings, a source of great

pride to Langsdorff. The responsibility for the long search for the elusive *Graf Spee* in the South Atlantic fell upon Royal Navy Forces G, H and K. Their success depended largely upon attacked merchantmen getting off their R-R-R signal and position. In fact, Langsdorff was better informed about British warship movements. He knew that the cruisers *Ajax*, *Achilles*, *Exeter* and *Cumberland* were operating off the South American coast; that the two heavy cruisers *Sussex* and *Shropshire* were off Cape Town and that the battle-cruiser *Renown* and aircraft-carrier *Ark Royal* were off West Africa.

As Commodore Harwood had predicted, Langsdorff determined to leave the mid-ocean patrol and, as if destiny was directing him to destruction, he set course for the River Plate estuary, attracted by the prospect of rich prizes. Harwood also headed for the estuary, leading one of the British Raider Hunting Forces searching the seas from the wastes of the North Atlantic to the southernmost tip of Latin America.

Commodore Harwood, as Officer Commanding the South American Division of the America and West Indies Squadron, flew his broad pennant in the 6985-ton 6 in-gun cruiser *Ajax*, commanded by Captain Charles H. L. Woodhouse. His two heavy 8 in-gun cruisers *Exeter* (Captain Frederick S. Bell) and the 9850-ton *Cumberland* were at Port Stanley. The 6 in-gun cruiser *Achilles* (Captain Edward Parry), of 7030 tons and

Above Commander of the *Graf Spee*, *Kapitan zur See* Hans Langsdorff. His ship was capable of winning the action, but inexplicably her captain failed her

Right The map shows the track of the *Graf Spee* before her arrival at the River Plate. Also shown are the plots of the positions where she sank the nine merchant ships

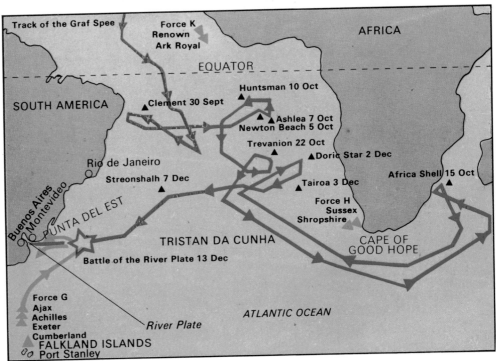

POCKET-BATTLESHIP
ADMIRAL GRAF SPEE (1934-39)

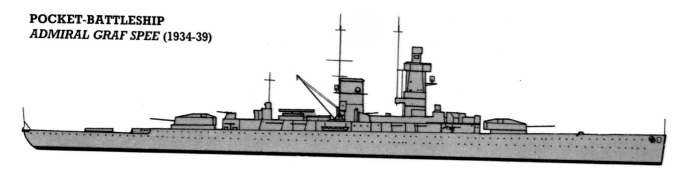

partly manned by 327 New Zealanders, was patrolling off Rio de Janeiro. *Ajax* had recently sailed from Port Stanley for the River Plate.

Harwood calculated after the *Doric Star* sinking that the raider could reach Rio by 12 December and be off the River Plate by the following day. Accordingly he ordered his cruisers to concentrate there. *Exeter* was instructed to leave Port Stanley on the 9th with *Achilles* to head south from Rio to join the flagship on the 10th. *Cumberland* had to remain in the Falklands to complete an important self-refit.

'Attack at once—day or night!'
By 0600 on 12 December the three cruisers were in company 240 km (150 miles) off the River Plate. The Commodore had long been considering the tactics his squadron should employ on encountering a pocket-battleship. At 1200 on 12 December, undaunted by their greatly superior gunpower, he made his intentions clear in a signal to his three captains: 'My policy with three cruisers in company versus one pocket-battleship: attack at once day or night.'

At dawn on 13 December the sea was calm with a light swell. As the light

strengthened the three grey British cruisers formed up in line ahead, *Ajax* leading *Achilles* and *Exeter*, 1800 m (2000 yards) apart. Soon after 0600, Leading Signalman Swanston on *Ajax*'s bridge sighted smoke over the horizon bearing 320 degrees. Harwood ordered *Exeter* to investigate. She swung out of line and at 0616 she signalled by lamp: 'I think it is a pocket-battleship,' and Captain Bell ordered Flag N hoisted to the yardarm: 'Enemy in sight.' *Graf Spee*, heading 155 degrees at 15 kts, logged an almost identical chart position. Langsdorff held the whiphand, for he had sighted the British ships 20 minutes before *Ajax* saw the smudge of smoke. The German stereoscopic main rangefinder measured a distance of 31 km (19.26 miles). By 0600 *Graf Spee* was cleared for action and the ships had resolved themselves into the unmistakable superstructures of HMS *Exeter* and possibly two destroyers.

Now, if ever, was the time for Langsdorff to turn about and refuse action. By maintaining course he committed a cardinal error. He went even further and contrary to instructions decided to attack, ordering full speed to close the range. Phase one of the Battle of the River Plate had begun even

Above The 12,100-ton *Graf Spee*, which was launched on 30 June 1934. She carried six 11 in guns, eight 5.9 in guns, and had a top speed of 27.7 kts. The crew totalled 1134 men.

Below The light cruiser HMS *Ajax*, which had a displacement of 6895 tons. She was armed with eight 6 in and eight 4 in AA guns. Top speed was 32.5 kts and her crew was 593 men

Bottom HMS *Exeter* was an 8390-ton heavy cruiser armed with six 8 in and four 4 in AA guns. Her top speed was 32 kts and her crew totalled 630

LIGHT CRUISER
HMS *AJAX* (1934-49)

HEAVY CRUISER
HMS *EXETER* (1929-42)

before the British cruisers had sighted the enemy. By now she had identified the 'destroyers' as *Ajax* and *Achilles*. Her only safeguard lay in crushing the opposition by destroying it or putting it to flight. At 0618 the two triple 11 in turrets opened fire with a thunderous crash.

When *Exeter* identified the pocket-battleship, Captain Bell hauled off to the west while Harwood led *Ajax* round to close the range. *Achilles* conformed to the flag-ship's movements throughout the action enabling the two light cruisers to concentrate their gunfire with great effect. All three ships increased sped, hoisted battle ensigns and fire was opened. *Exeter*'s 8 in guns opened at 0620, *Achilles*' 6 in at 0621 and *Ajax*'s two minutes later. The range was then about 18 km (10.8 miles), Langsdorff had made no effort to maintain his range advantage and he now found himself, as Harwood intended, confronted with two divisions and the problem of whether to divide his main armament to engage them both—or to leave one unengaged. Initially, *Graf Spee* engaged both but very soon shifted fire of all six 11 in guns to *Exeter*. Her accuracy was formidable and remained so throughout the day.

Exeter's 'A' and 'B' turrets opened fire at 0620 with 'Y' turret following two and a half minutes later. Full speed was ordered at 0620. With his third salvo, the gunnery officer, Lieutenant Commander Richard B. Jennings, straddled *Graf Spee* and prospects looked promising. But *Exeter* herself was under fire and *Graf Spee*'s third

main salvo straddled the British ship. A minute later *Graf Spee*'s eighth salvo struck an almost decisive blow: within seconds *Exeter* was transformed from an efficient fighting unit into an uncontrollable machine. 'B' turret took a direct hit between the two gun barrels, putting it and eight of the crew out of action. Splinters swept the bridge killing or wounding nearly everyone there; the wheelhouse was smashed, vital communications cut. Captain Bell, wounded himself, was compelled to retire to the after-conning position where a human chain of command was set up.

While the 11 in salvoes were being directed at *Exeter*, Langsdorff employed his eight 5.9 in guns against the 16 6 in guns of the two light cruisers, whose accuracy was such that the pocket-battleship shifted fire from the *Exeter* to bring her 11 in guns to bear on *Achilles* and *Ajax*. *Exeter*'s shooting astonished the *Graf Spee*'s officers both for its accuracy and in particular for the rapidity of each following salvo. Her fifth salvo scored a direct hit but the shell passed through the upper part of the bridge without exploding and caused little damage. Another 8 in shell passed through the 14 cm (5½ in) armoured deck and finally exploded amidships. At 0632 the damaged *Exeter*, under severe pressure from the accurate German gunnery, fired her three starboard torpedo tubes. A few minutes later *Graf Spee* made a heavy alteration of course to port and steered north-west under cover of smoke.

From this moment on the battle became a

This chart shows the complex of manoeuvres taken by the ships during the battle of the River Plate. The red line shows the track of the *Graf Spee*, and the green and blue lines illustrate how the Royal Navy ships harried and worried the much more powerful German vessel, known as a pocket-battleship, until she sought refuge in Montevideo. Her next voyage was short and her last

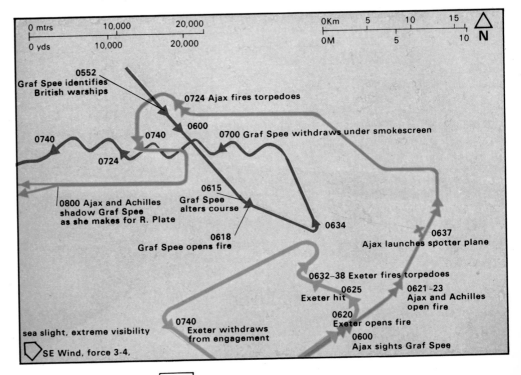

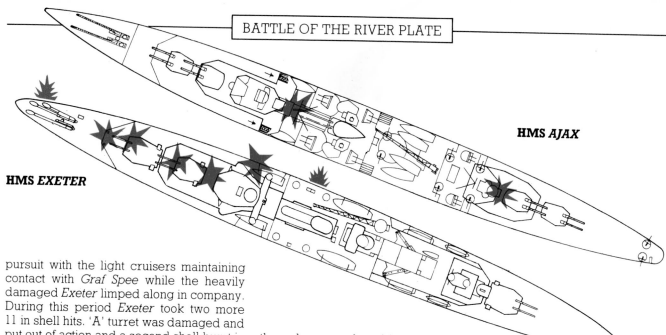

HMS AJAX

HMS EXETER

pursuit with the light cruisers maintaining contact with *Graf Spee* while the heavily damaged *Exeter* limped along in company. During this period *Exeter* took two more 11 in shell hits. 'A' turret was damaged and put out of action and a second shell burst in the Chief Petty Officer's position amidships, starting a fierce fire. It was this shell which created the most damage; the 4 in magazine was flooded by burst water mains; all compass repeaters were out of action and Captain Bell handled the cruiser using a whaler's compass. The ship's upperworks were pierced with splinters, dead and dying littered the decks. Lieutenant Commander Jennings, now stationed on the after searchlight platform, kept the single remaining 'Y' turret in action under local control. Captain Bell kept adjusting course to keep the turret bearing on the target. *Exeter* took another shell hit under the fo'c'sle, suffered flooding of several compartments and took a seven degree list to starboard. Ablaze, she had taken heavy punishment and was close to being destroyed.

At 0640, when one of *Graf Spee*'s 11 in turrets was being directed against the light cruisers, a shell near-missed *Achilles*, bursting on impact with the sea. Hundreds of splinters penetrated her thin bridge plating and the armour of the Director Control Tower, killing four ratings. Captain Parry and the Chief Yeoman on the bridge were slightly wounded and a splinter severed the halyard for the White Ensign: the battle continued to be fought under the New Zealand flag at the mainmast.

At 0725 *Ajax* received an 11 in shell hit on the after superstructure: the shell passed through several cabins, wrecking the machinery below 'X' turret and burst in the Commodore's sleeping cabin. Damage was sustained by the 'Y' turret barbette, jamming it. Thus one shell effectively put both 'X' and 'Y' turrets out of action, killing and wounding many of the guns' crews. By now *Exeter* was out of the fight, her speed reduced, falling astern of the action, fires raging, 61 officers and ratings killed. *Ajax*, the flagship, had been reduced to only half her main armament. Only *Achilles* remained practically undamaged.

Was Langsdorff correct?

Langsdorff's tactics—British and German naval experts are agreed on this point—are difficult to understand because he should have headed southward to finish off *Exeter* before turning his attention upon the two light cruisers. Yet he deliberately allowed *Exeter* to escape, then pointlessly sought sanctuary in a neutral harbour. Harwood continued to harry *Graf Spee*, and by 0728 the range was down to only 7 km (4.54 miles). *Graf Spee* was now being subjected to a deluge of accurate 6 in gunfire and the pocket-battleship even brought into action some of her six 4.1 in AA guns against the

Deck plans of *Graf Spee*, *Ajax* and *Exeter*, showing the main shell hits on each vessel. The larger red flashes represent heavy calibre rounds. *Graf Spee* was hit in both 11 in gun turrets and a large hole was punctured in her bows on the waterline. Her port ammunition hoist, conning tower, port No. 3 5.9 in gun shield sustained hits. The forward AA control post was hit and communications and searchlights put out of action. The crew suffered 37 killed and 57 wounded. *Ajax* took an 11 in shell hit on her 'X' turret ammunition lobby, a second 11 in shell hit the main topmast. She was also hit near the bridge. Two of *Exeter*'s 8 in gun turrets were hit and she was holed in the bows, taking seven 11 in hits altogether. They killed 61 officers and men

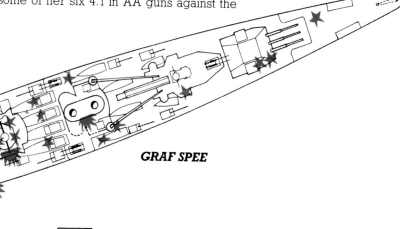

GRAF SPEE

Above HMS *Achilles* before the action. She displaced 7030 tons and had eight 6 in guns. After World War 2 she served in the Indian Navy

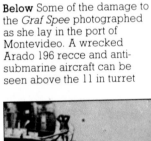

Below Some of the damage to the *Graf Spee* photographed as she lay in the port of Montevideo. A wrecked Arado 196 recce and anti-submarine aircraft can be seen above the 11 in turret

cruisers. *Graf Spee*, now on a westerly course and clearly heading for the River Plate estuary, was still maintaining accurate fire, one of her last salvoes, at 0738, bringing down *Ajax*'s mainmast with all its radio aerials. Harwood decided to break off the day action, carry out the traditional cruiser duty of shadowing, and close in again after dark. The light cruisers turned away to the east under cover of smoke but continued to maintain contact. *Exeter* set course for the Falklands and at 1000 *Cumberland* sailed from the Falklands for the River Plate to take her place.

Langsdorff made no attempt to pursue Harwood as the cruisers broke off action. He headed for Montevideo in Uruguay at 22 kts and took stock. Senior Surgeon Dr Kartzendorff reported one officer and 35 ratings killed and 61 others wounded. In no way did these casualties reduce the fighting capacity of a ship with a complement of 1134, but the supply of 11 in shells was only

186—31 per gun, not enough for a battle.

Damage-control reports revealed a considerable amount of minor damage by 17 6 in shell hits from *Ajax* and *Achilles* and more serious damage by the three 8 in hits from *Exeter*. The direction-finding apparatus and the equipment for purifying lubricating oil was damaged, as were the forward ammunition hoists. The armour belt and armoured deck had been penetrated with two holes in the bows, the largest measuring 1.9 m (6 ft) wide. More important was slight damage to the main range-finder, foretop, torpedo-ranging device and the fire-fighting equipment.

One hit was from a practice shell from *Achilles*. It hit aft, killed two ratings, passed through half a dozen cabins and came to rest in the berth of a petty officer—still identifiable as a drill round! The large hole in the bows was serious because *Graf Spee* would ship water if she made a dash for Germany. Langsdorff said: 'Our damage cannot be repaired with the means available on board. We must run into port somewhere for repairs.'

Ajax and *Achilles* continued their shadowing for the rest of the day, *Achilles* followed close to the coast. *Ajax* remained to the south to cover a possible doubling back at dusk. At 1915 *Graf Spee* fired two accurate salvoes and at 2048 another three. Sporadic firing finished at 2142 and the pursuit and shadowing phase of the battle ended when *Graf Spee* anchored off Montevideo at 2350.

While the battle and pursuit were in progress the Royal Navy was making dispositions to engage *Graf Spee* whenever she should quit Montevideo. *Cumberland* joined her consorts at 2200 on 14 December after steaming 1600 km (1000 miles) in 34 hours. The 8 in cruisers *Dorsetshire* and *Shropshire*, carrier *Ark Royal*, battlecruiser *Renown* and modern cruiser *Neptune* were all directed to the River Plate. But this overwhelming strength could not concentrate there before 19 December.

'The trap of Montevideo'

Meanwhile, Langsdorff was the centre of an unprecedented diplomatic storm in what he later called 'the trap of Montevideo'. He had secured a 72-hour extension over the 24-hour permissible stay of a warship in a neutral port. British objections were more academic than real for they had no wish to force *Graf Spee* to sea before the 19th, and the ploy of sailing a British merchant ship each day was adopted. International Law provided that merchantmen leaving port had to be given a head start of 24 hours over an enemy warship.

On 16 December Langsdorff reported to Berlin—erroneously—his belief that the British concentration of warships already lay in wait outside the harbour. *Grossadmiral* Eric Raeder, Commander-in-Chief of the German Navy, discussed this naval dilemma with Adolf Hitler and they agreed that an attempted fighting breakout to Buenos Aires, in Argentina, was the proper course of action, failing which scuttling would be preferable to internment.

At 1815 on 17 December Langsdorff conned *Graf Spee* out of harbour. Soon after the ship was outside the three mile limit she stopped and anchored. Tugs approached. The ensign was lowered. Six fuses were lit. Boats—the last one containing Langsdorff—headed away from *Graf Spee* across the River Plate towards Buenos Aires. Six violent explosions shattered the quiet of evening. The pocket-battleship *Graf Spee* exploded like a volcano and settled in the shallows of the estuary, surely deserving a more dignified end than a scuttling. She burned like a pyre about 6 km (4 miles) from land.

Lieutenant H. Dietrich found Langsdorff the following morning. He had shot himself.

Below The wrecked and scuttled *Graf Spee* lying in shallow water after steaming from Montevideo on 17 December 1939. Her captain laid six torpedo warheads in the ammunition hoists and lit the fuses before being last to leave his ship

The Germans launched their offensive in the West on 10 May 1940, and on 12 May Brigadier Douglas Pratt was ordered to move his brigade forward into the Brussels area. Just after the 1st Army Tank Brigade had completed its move, seven German Panzer divisions broke right through the French defences. On 20 May General Heinz Guderian's 19 Panzer Corps reached the sea west of Abbeville and turned northwards towards the Channel ports.

Heavy German infantry attacks had failed to penetrate the front of the British Expeditionary Forces (BEF), but on 16 May General Gaston Billotte, commander of the First Group of Armies (which included the BEF), ordered a withdrawal to the line of the river Escaut (or Scheldt) which was to be reached on the night of 18-19 May. British General Headquarters promptly ordered 1st Army Tank Brigade to Tournai.

By 1100 on 17 May the whole brigade was at Ath. On 18 May the brigade clanked through bombed-out Tournai into Orchies 26 km (16 miles) SE of Lille. On the evening

of 18 May the German 7th Panzer Division, the most advanced formation on the inner flank of the armoured thrust, had reached Cambrai, 38 km (24 miles) south of Orchies. Here, General Irwin Rommel halted them, his intention to continue his advance on the evening of 19 May and seize the high ground SE of Arras. The British sent light tank patrols towards Cambrai but they failed to gain contact with the enemy. During the night of 19-20 May 7th Panzer Division moved 40 km (25 miles) to the west nearer Arras.

Early on the morning of 20 May 1st Army Tank Brigade and the 5th Division were ordered to join 50th Northumberland Division in the Vimy area, to the north of Arras, in preparation for an attack. This force was to be known as 'Frankforce' under command of Major-General Franklyn, GOC 5th Division.

Then, General Sir Edmund Ironside, Chief of the Imperial General Staff, visited General Gort, Commander-in-Chief BEF, and told him that only an attack with his

The progress of the two British tank columns can be seen as they swung south of Arras. General Rommel was convinced that a superior force was attacking him

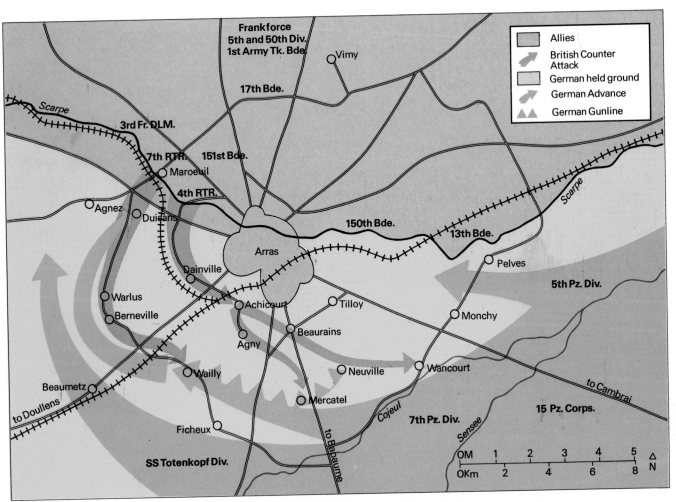

PANZER III AUSF. E

whole force in the direction of Amiens, supported if possible by the neighbouring French troops, could free the BEF from encirclement. If Gort thought this possible he would give him an order to attack at once and he would try to get the French near him to conform. Gort could not agree. Seven of his nine divisions were fighting on the Scheldt, and even if they could be disengaged their withdrawal would leave a gap between the Belgians and the BEF through which the enemy would penetrate. There were also strong enemy columns moving round the British right flank between Arras and the Somme, and Gort only had four days' supplies and enough ammunition for one more battle.

On the night of 20 May Franklyn was informed by French First Army that their

attack towards Cambrai could not be mounted until 22 May. Franklyn did not feel that this had any direct bearing on his operation. But it had been forgotten by GHQ, for after Ironside's visit, a big Anglo-French counter-stroke to the south was being envisaged, and that, together with the leading brigade of Major-General Giffard Le Martel's 50th Division, had taken over the stretch of the Scarpe east of Arras from the French.

Franklyn deployed the major part of his two divisions to strengthen the defences of Arras and the Scarpe, because from the wording of his orders the support of the garrison of Arras appeared the major task and road blocking to the south a subsidiary operation. GHQ, however, were thinking of

Above The German Panzer III, Ausf. ('Mk') E. It weighed 20 tons and had a crew of five. The main armament was a 37 mm gun, with three MGs. It could reach 40 k/h (25 mph), with a range of 160 km (100 miles)

Below The British Army's counterpart, the Matilda, Infantry Tank Mk I. This AFV was intended for infantry support only, and was armed with a .5 in Vickers MG. It weighed only 11 tons and could travel at 10 k/h (8 mph) for 125 km (80 miles)

INFANTRY TANK MK. 1 'MATILDA'

Above Major-General Martel, who led the British columns at Arras.

Below General Rommel examining a tactical map during a military exercise. He commanded the 7th ('Ghost') Panzer Division. He lost many men and much equipment at Arras. Standing in the foreground is his ADC, Lt Most, who was killed by Rommel's side during the action at Arras

a British and French attack to the south.

Fifth and 50th Divisions had only two infantry brigades each instead of three. The 151st Brigade was sent to strengthen the garrison of Arras and hold the line of the Scarpe immediately east of the city. The 151st Brigade was to support 1st Army Tank Brigade in the attack.

First Army Tank Brigade moved to Vimy, some 48 km (30 miles) from Orchies, through Carvin and Lens. The move took place under frequent air attack along roads jammed with refugees and troops. The last tanks reached Vimy at about 0500 on 21 May. They had now covered 195 km (120 miles) in five days. As a result, out of 77 Mark I infantry tanks and 23 Mk IIs, only 58 Mk Is and 16 Mk IIs were serviceable on their worn-out tracks. The tired 151st Infantry Brigade, consisting of three Durham Light Infantry (DLI) Territorial battalions, marched into Vimy during the early hours of 21 May.

The orders for Major-General Martel were to 'clear and capture the area south of the river Scarpe from inclusive southern outskirts of Arras including Pelves and Monchy (about 8 km (5 miles) to the east) thence line of Cojeul river as far as road Arras-Bapaume.'

Britain's first mobile tank operation

Martel organized his force into two mixed but balanced columns: each of a tank battalion, an infantry battalion, a field artillery and an anti-tank (AT) battery, an infantry AT platoon and a scout platoon for recce. It was the first time that the British Army had used such mobile battle groups in war. The third infantry battalion of 151st Brigade was to be retained in support of the attacking units, totalling 74 tanks and fewer than 3500 men.

Rommel was informed on 20 May that some British and French divisions had moved into his area, so put his force into a defensive position south of Arras. He had 180 tanks to deploy. The 25th Panzer Regiment attacked at 1300 and 800 m (half a mile) east of Wailly they came under heavy fire from the north.

At this time it was apparent that the British infantry would be half an hour late in reaching their start line. Brigadier Douglas H. Pratt accordingly proposed that the attack should be postponed; but Martel decided that the tanks should start without waiting for the infantry. Shortly after 1315 the tanks moved off towards the start line. But this was no longer relevant. Maroeuil was being heavily shelled when the right column passed through it at 1430 to cross the Scarpe. French tanks advancing on the

right reported enemy tanks advancing farther west—part of Rommel's 25th Panzer Regiment starting their move to the north-west. The infantry of the right column caught up after 6 km (4 miles), some being left in Duisans to guard prisoners and hold the village against attack.

The infantry captured Warlus by 1530, then Berneville, a mile farther on. An advance guard of tanks, with some DLI, moved on to the Arras-Doullens road—the original start line!

Here, the surprised German defence began to stiffen, inflicting 50 per cent losses on the DLI. At Wailly the crisis came at about 1600 as Rommel arrived. His artillery-men began to desert their guns, leaving with retreating infantry. But the General reorganized his artillery and began picking off the British tanks to such an extent that they gave up the unequal gun battle and fell back on Warlus.

The stronger left column, starting at 1130, fought its way deeper into German lines, capturing four villages quickly. The tanks annihilated a motor transport (MT) column in Dainville and then overran a dis-heartened AT battery which had seen its 37 mm armour piercing (AP) shells fail to penetrate the Matilda tanks' armour at 455 m (500 yd).

The 4th Royal Tank Regiment (RTR) pushed south of Beauvais to Mercatel at 1600, but that was the limit of their success as Rommel built up a gun-line that sealed off the battlefield.

Night tank duel

Rommel ordered 25th Panzer Regiment to attack southwards to hit the British armour in flank and rear. The fighting culminated with a night tank duel between six German medium tanks and 11 British, ending in the formers' retreat. The German counter-attack inflicted losses of seven tanks and six AT guns, but suffered the loss of three precious Panzer IVs and six IIIs. During the night the British forces withdrew.

The first British tank attack of the war penetrated a depth of 16 km (10 miles) and had been a limited tactical success. Casualties were 700 men (400 prisoners of war (POWs)) and about 20 tanks. But in strategic terms Arras was a British victory out of all proportion to the forces committed. Rommel described Arras as a 'very heavy battle against hundreds of enemy tanks and following infantry'—he thought he was being attacked by vastly superior forces.

In retrospect, it has become clear that a desperately improvised attack by a handful of British tanks at Arras contributed to the miracle of Dunkirk.

THE FALL OF FRANCE

While the BEF and other Allied troops were being evacuated from Dunkirk, the German tanks which had halted on the Aa canal were redeployed to face south-west as part of the invasion of Central France. In all the Germans deployed 143 full-strength divisions, seven more than on 10 May when Belgium and Holland had to be fought as well as France.

On this 360 km (225 mile) front the French under General Maxime Weygand had five armies with a total strength of only 43 depleted and unmotorized infantry divisions. The Maginot Line enabled 17 fortress divisions to hold the other 355 km (220 miles). There were three battered armoured divisions, mustering just 250 modern tanks, deployed in three groups for

The path of the powerful German thrust deep into France in June 1940. A token armoured resistance was put up by French reserves but they were quickly swamped

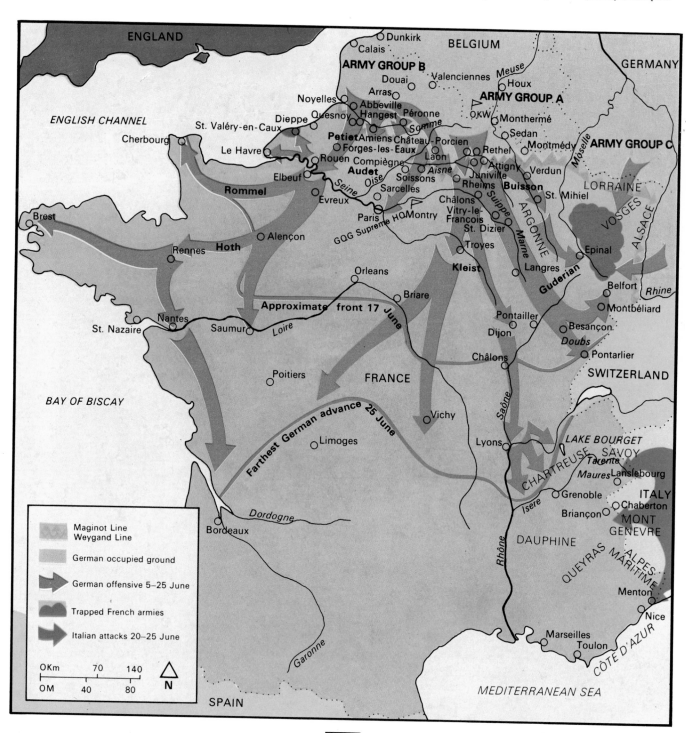

Top A French Hotchkiss H39 Light Tank in flames, one of the out-gunned and out-numbered AFVs which faced the Panzers

Left A French Private of the 14th Infantry Division, very similar to the soldiers of World War 1

Right This French tank crewman is facing at best a POW cage. It took only ten days to eliminate all the French tank units

counter-attack against some 2500 Panzers. The necessarily token British contribution of 30,000 fighting men came in 51st (Highland) Infantry Division and the skeleton 1st Armoured Division (fewer than 150 tanks).

Against the Luftwaffe's 3500 aircraft the French had 450 modern fighters and 65 bombers left, with some obsolete aircraft. The RAF was flying sorties from England, but none of its 600 home defence fighters were based in France. On 3 June the Luftwaffe sent 300 bombers against French airfields and aircraft factories around Paris, an air prelude to the ground offensive.

France's last barrier

The Weygand Line was to be the last barrier and the battle a gesture of honour for future historians. Indeed, Weygand said 'No methodical retreat is possible with such a numerical inferiority.'

Despite this the French soldiers shared none of these misgivings. They had suffered losses but found a new determination. They were deployed in a series of 'hedgehog' positions in some depth, but there were not enough men nor enough AP and AT mines to make it work. They held the woods and villages covering the roads and dug in the 75 mm guns. One third of the artillery was to be used in the AT role. On 5 June, the day after Dunkirk ended, Weygand issued an Order of the Day: 'The Battle of France has begun. The order is to defend our positions without thought of retreat. Officers, non-commissioned officers and soldiers . . . the Fate of our Country, the safeguarding of her Liberties . . . depend on your tenacity.'

The dawn of 5 June was mild. On a 195 km (120 mile) front from the Channel to Laon a massed air and artillery bombardment churned the Weygand Line into dust and smoke. The Germans had planned their attack in two phases. On the left the tanks of Army Group B would attack on 5 June, followed four days later by those of Army Group A on the right.

Almost at once the Germans ran into severe resistance. Both at Amiens and Peronne 14 and 16 Panzer Corps failed to break out from their bridgehead. The following day the French still held firm, aided by a timely 50-bomber strike, they had disabled 65 per cent of Colonel General Ewald von Kleist's attacking armour. In the centre, infantry of the German Ninth Army got over the Aillette Canal and across the Chemin des Dames to the Aisne at Soissons.

Rommel breaks out

On the right, Rommel had broken out and advanced 30 km (20 miles), partly at night, after fierce fighting west of Amiens. The next day he reached Forges-les-Eaux, 59 km (37 miles) south of the Somme, and thus split the French Tenth Army in two. On 8 June Rommel took Elbeuf on the Seine, reaching the sea two days later. He had broken through by the simple tactic of taking his vehicles off the roads covered by the 'hedgehogs' and driving across country.

The French left flank had been unhinged and at 1800 on 6 June Weygand ordered 3rd Army Group to fall back. Many formations were cut off and though surrounded they continued to fight. Three regiments of 167th Division in Seventh Army were overrun south of Amiens but the surrounded gunners took on Kleist's tanks over open sights. The 19th Divisional Reconnaissance Group repeatedly counter-attacked only to be swamped by the German 29th Motorized Division. By 17 June 16th Division had been reduced to four out of 12 infantry battalions.

Rommel swung left to capture the Channel ports. In one day he drove 95 km (60 miles) to reach the sea and began to push back up the coast. On 12 June he captured Le Havre, then set up an all-time record for a day's tank thrust on the 17th when he raced 240 km (150 miles) to take Cherbourg and its garrison of 30,000 men.

During their blitzkrieg through France the German Army could mass huge numbers of artillery, such as the 105 mm howitzer shown here. It formed 75 per cent of their guns. This battery is lined up on the River Aisne. The artillery was supported by tanks and aircraft, which the French lacked

Right A German tripod-mounted MG34 waiting for a target. This MG saw long and successful service with the Wehrmacht during World War 2

Below When General Maxime Weygand was given command of the French Army, taking over from General Maurice Gamelin, who had become ineffectual and exhausted, the 73-year-old commander knew that the battle was already lost. But he made the struggle more difficult for the Germans than the battles in the north

Weygand makes a 'supreme appeal'

Four days after the Somme attack, the French Fourth Army on the right of 3rd Army Group came under severe bombardment. Weygand issued a 'supreme appeal': 'The order remains, for each one, to fight without thought of giving ground . . . where the Command has placed him. . . . We have come to the last quarter of an hour. Stand firm!' They were to stand firm against the combined strength of eight Panzer divisions, from *Panzergruppe Guderian* to Kleist's *Panzergruppe*.

General Guderian records that the opening assault by German infantry at Chateau-Porcien on 9 June only established a bridgehead 1½-2 km (1-1½ miles) deep after five hours of bitter fighting against the French 2nd Infantry Division, while east of Rethel the attacks had to be called off.

Three German Twelfth Army infantry divisions attacked at 0600 after several hours barrage. By 1300 they had been flung back by counter-attacks that took 800 prisoners in the day. Next morning the French held on unflinchingly but 36th Division inflicted 1000 casualties on the German 26th Division during 9 June; they had been forced too far back and had to reform.

Guderian seized the opportunity of the shallow bridgeheads at Chateau-Porcien to switch 39 Panzer Corps from Rethel and tanks were rafted over the river during the night for an attack at 0630 on 10 June. By 1300 the *Panzergruppe* had reached Juniville. Then the French advanced 3 km (2 miles), destroying about 100 armoured fighting vehicles (AFVs) and rescuing an encircled infantry regiment before numbers told. But 2nd Panzer had crossed the Seine and had reached the outskirts of Rheims.

With the Weygand Line ruptured along its entire length the French Government began to evacuate Paris on 10 June. The honour of taking the French capital fell to the infantry, as the Panzers streamed past to the east and west. On the morning of 14 June, men of the 87th Infantry Division began to enter the city.

Parisians awoke to see the swastika flying from public buildings. Armoured car and loudspeaker vans patrolled the streets and by breakfast Paris had become the fifth national capital in two months to fall to Germany.

The French had lost 25 divisions since 5 June and fighter strength was down to 180, but still they managed to put up some spirited resistance. Chalons-sur-Marne was reached by 2nd Panzer on 12 June and its recce troops captured a bridge intact, but as they crossed it French engineers fired explosive charges.

While Paris was being occupied, 1st Panzer captured St Dizier. Guderian was close behind and urged the division forward to take Langres with 3000 POWs after driving 105 km (66 miles) on 15 June. As the German advance accelerated so French resistance deteriorated.

The French begin to crumble

By 15 June the three French army groups were being steadily fragmented or out-flanked. The German Seventh Army was finally crossing the Rhine and carving out a bridgehead in Alsace. Only on a line south of Paris, where the German pressure was lightest, were the French withdrawing in any order. East and SE of Paris Fourth and part of Sixth Armies had virtually disappeared. The three French Army group headquarters had been pushed back so fast that they were now almost as far south as their GHQ at Vichy. The senior commanders regarded continued resistance as impossible. But the Germans pressed on to reach the Loire. Alencon was reached on the 17th and the way was open to the naval base at Brest. Nantes fell on 19 June, but the Germans ran into stiff resistance at Saumur, the 2300 cadets of the French Cavalry School holding off the Germans for two days.

On 16 June French Prime Minister Paul Reynard resigned and called on 84-year-old Marshal Henri Petain to form a new Cabinet. He was pledged to end the fighting with an immediate armistice. But Guderian's Panzers still had things to do despite Petain's cease-fire order. They captured 40,000 prisoners at Epinal, and on the 20th encircled 2nd Army Group and Second Army, 400,000 men laying down their arms.

The *Panzergruppe* had captured a further 250,000 prisoners as well as a vast number of guns and vehicles. Then France suffered a greater humiliation—the signing of the armistice at 1850 on 22 June in the railway coach at Rethondes, near Compienge, where Germany had signed in 1918. The military outcome of the Battle for France was a foregone conclusion. German army losses up to Dunkirk had been 61,200, but the conquest of France added 95,300. France lost nearly a million prisoners with some 170,000 killed and wounded.

A grim silence descended on France, over which the swastika was to fly for four years and two months. But huge numbers of German troops were needed to hold the vast French territory and control the dedicated and brave Resistance groups.

Hands raised in surrender, French troops stand dejectedly while their victors of the Wehrmacht search them for hidden weapons and any papers that might be of Intelligence interest. They were probably relieved of any personal valuables at the same time, a reprehensible practice but one adopted by all troops at some time or another

As 340,000 men of the British Expeditionary Force together with other retreating soldiers were taken off the bullet- and shrapnel-riddled beaches of Dunkirk, the war was not going well for Britain. After the brilliant victory by the Royal Navy over the pocket-battleship *Graf Spee* the previous December, the war on land was becoming grim. The Continent of Europe was almost totally in Hitler's grasp, the British Isles being the main stumbling block to full domination by the German Army. However, Hitler's avowed objective was still the vast expanse of Russia.

Since no approach had come from Britain in seeking to avoid invasion by force, Germany made her own offer—nothing more than a demand for total surrender: strangely, it took Britain three days before rejecting it. So Hitler and his High

A stick of bombs toppling out from the bomb bay of a Heinkel 111. This medium bomber had cut its teeth over Spain during the Civil War and was used in large numbers over Britain in World War 2.

Command sat down on 1 August to finalize plans for a quick blitzkrieg-type assault across the Channel, calling it Operation Sealion. The date for the operation was set for 15 September 1940.

'Eliminate the RAF!'

But before any move across the Channel was attempted the vital point upon which all the German armed forces were agreed was that the Royal Air Force had first to be eliminated. Hitler wanted the invasion of Britain to be quick and painless, with as few casualties as possible to his soldiers. His next and last objective would be Russia and he knew that all his manpower would be needed for that formidable task.

This, then, is the background to what is known as the Battle of Britain and it was fought in the air over London and the Home Counties. Before the invasion proper, the Luftwaffe had already been engaged in attacking selected British targets, using bases sited along the French coast and employing up to 70 bombers at a time. It was useful experience for those aircrews recruited since the Spanish Civil War and whose battle experience had been against fairly thin opposition. The RAF's losses during the time it had operated as part of the British Expeditionary Force in France

had been totally unacceptable: some 250 fighters were lost in the six weeks before mid-June, which prompted Air Chief Marshal Sir Hugh Dowding, Air Officer Commander-in-Chief Fighter Command, to appeal to the Prime Minister, pleading that insufficient aircraft were being held in reserve. It led to Winston Churchill giving instructions on 19 May that no further RAF squadrons would be posted to French bases.

The decision that saved Britain

With the benefit of hindsight, this decision probably saved the war for Britain and her Allies, for had the RAF received such a battering that it became terminally weakened the invasion would have gone ahead, with dreadfully predictable results.

So, the lines were drawn. In Northern Germany and the Lowlands was *Loftflotte II*, commanded by Field Marshal Albert Kesselring; Field Marshal Hugo Sparrle headed *Luftflotte III* in North and Western France, while in Norway and Denmark General Hans-Jurgen Stumpff led a smaller force, *Luftflotte V*.

The combined strength of these German air fleets totalled about 3000 aircraft, some third of which were fighters, while the bombers were the He11, Do17 and the

Above A stricken Spitfire rears up, to stall then spiral down in flames

Below A Spitfire squadron lined up on the grass at Biggin Hill, Kent, one of the front-line airfields during the Battle of Britain

This gaggle of Ju87 Stukas is not flying over Britain, but seeking out guerrilla targets in Yugoslavia later in World War 2. The Stuka was tried over Britain, but it was no match for the Spitfires and Hurricanes and was shot down in unacceptable numbers. Goering soon withdrew it for he could afford to lose neither aircraft nor trained operational pilots

newer Ju88. The dreaded Ju87 divebomber was also present in numbers.

What had the RAF to oppose this threat? Although the losses in France had been serious (by 4 June there were fewer than 450 Spitfires and Hurricanes available), replacements had been rushed forward and by the opening of the Battle of Britain on 11 August the RAF was able to muster over 700 machines, with about 300 in reserve. This was due mainly to the energy and drive of Lord Beaverbrook, newly appointed Minister of Aircraft Production.

It was against this background that RAF Fighter Command awaited the expected aerial onslaught. Under Dowding, the command was divided into four groups, Nos 10, 11, 12 and 13. No. 11 Group, operating from airfields in South East England and headed by Air Vice Marshal Keith Park, a New Zealand Scot, would be in the front line and responsible for defending London, its own airfields, the radar chain and the coast along which any invasion attempt could be expected.

Park had an average of 19 squadrons comprising about 200 serviceable fighters. Thirteen of his squadrons were equipped with Hurricanes, only six with Spitfires. Dowding's resources, including No. 11 Group, were 25 squadrons of Hurricanes and 20 of Spitfires. Dowding knew that after including six Blenheim squadrons, mainly equipped for experimental night fighting and two squadrons of Boulton Paul Defiants, he could muster a total of about 700 fighters of varying performance. Across the Channel and the North Sea Germany had *Luftflotten II*, *III* and *V*. They comprised 900 Me109 fighters, 300 twin-engine Me110 fighters, 300 Ju87 divebombers and a thousand Do17, He111 and Ju88 medium bombers.

The initial action on the first day of the battle was typical of Britain's plight. Shortly before 1400 on 10 July six Hurricanes of

No. 32 Squadron from Biggin Hill, Kent, were approaching their patrol line 3050 m (10,000 ft) above a convoy off Dover. The Hurricane pilots saw 'waves of enemy bombers in boxes of six,' reported Acting Sub-Lieutenant G. G. R. Bulmer, RN, on loan from the Fleet Air Arm because of the RAF's shortage of operationally trained fighter pilots.

Luftwaffe's defensive cylinder formation
The Hurricanes divided into two sections, one of three aircraft diving into a hundred of the enemy. A further 12 Hurricanes and eight Spitfires from four other squadrons were hastening to the scene. As the Spitfires arrived, 100 enemy bombers and fighters had spiralled themselves into three layers, forming a cylinder over the convoy. On top were Me109s, in the middle Me110s and below them Do17 bombers. Climbing to 4000 m (13,000 ft), an advantage of 300 m (1000 ft) over the 109s, the Spitfires dived into the cylinder. By sea level most of them were out of ammunition. Four Hurricanes were lost as against four enemy fighters, but only one ship was sunk.

Losses which led to the need to reinforce front-line squadrons began to mount in mid-August, especially from 13 August, the day selected by Germany as 'Eagle Day', the start of the all-out offensive planned to win air supremacy over Southern England and thus create the conditions which would allow for the invasion on 15 September.

It would take, according to the German High Command after being briefed by Marshal Hermann Goering, about a week to drive the RAF from the skies over South East England.

There is no doubt that invasion was a definite objective. Luftwaffe bomber crews had orders not to bomb South Coast ports, and even before France fell the Germans carefully avoided dropping bombs on French ports where invasion fleets could be mustered.

In the next phase, in August, the Stukas were committed early against British airfields and coastal defences but despite massive fighter protection the *Stuka-gruppen* were cut to ribbons. The slow-moving dive-bombers proved easy prey for the RAF's Spitfires and Hurricanes. They were withdrawn from the battle.

Tea-time party for the RAF
On 13 August, No. 609 Squadron recorded in its Operations Book: '13 Spitfires left Warmwell for a memorable tea time party over Lyme Bay and an unlucky day for the species Ju87 in which no less than 14 suffered destruction or damage in a record

squadron bag which also included five of the escorting Mes.' An Me109 could outdive a Hurricane and a Stuka might, but there was no escaping a tail-hugging Spitfire unless it was 'jumped' itself. By sunset on Eagle Day Dowding's Hurricanes and Spitfires had flown 700 sorties, some as many as three times each, to defend Britain from 1485 sorties flown by the enemy, one-third of which were bomber attacks. In the post-war count the Luftwaffe lost 45 aircraft to the RAF's 13.

But the defenders faced an even bigger test on 15 August, the first and only day on which the RAF had to counter the concerted attacks from all three *Luftflotten*. Hermann Goering reckoned that the RAF would have to abandon its airfields in Southern England. No. 12 Group, north of London, did think that the battle might be fought the more effectively from the rear. Repeated take-offs and landings exposed Air Vice Marshal Park's southern-based Hurricanes and Spitfires to destruction on the ground while taking on fuel and ammunition. Moreover, pilots operating from some of No. 11 Group's forward airfields invariably needed to climb inland away from the approaching enemy waves in order to gain sufficient altitude to turn and fight.

The employment of *Luftflotte V* on 15 August, however, introduced a new and contrary factor. Given sufficient radar notice, the fighter squadrons of No. 13 Group, north of No. 12 Group, had to intercept raiders crossing the North Sea. This was a more hazardous flight for the enemy than that over the narrower English Channel. It also gave longer radar warning of the approaching force, 65 He111 bombers and 35 Me110s 161 km (100 miles) out to sea from the East Coast of Scotland. No. 13 Group scrambled three Spitfire squadrons and one of Hurricanes. From

A German war correspondent took this photograph through the front nose-cone of an He111 during the Battle of Britain. The Luftwaffe air-gunner is aiming badly at a Spitfire that has dived through the German bomber formation

Right From the front: a Spitfire V; Spitfire IIA; Hurricane IIC; and two Spitfires Mk XIX. The photograph was taken after the Battle of Britain, for Mk XIXs were a later variant

their advantage of altitude, an advantage so frequently denied the defenders of South East England, the Spitfires dived into the enemy formations. The Luftwaffe lost eight bombers and seven fighters, the RAF none.

Churchill's famous eulogy

At this stage of the battle, as the Luftwaffe savaged Dowding's front-line airfields, to escape by parachute to fight again became a paramount part of a British fighter-pilot's skill. On 18 August, for instance, the RAF destroyed 71 enemy aircraft for the loss of 27 fighters, but only ten pilots. Nevertheless, in the previous ten days Dowding lost 183 fighters in the air and 30 destroyed on the ground, with 94 pilots killed or missing and 60 wounded, many seriously burned. Dowding repeatedly asked the Air Staff to release pilots from Bomber and Coastal Commands. He was eventually and somewhat grudgingly allowed 20 bomber pilots and 33 Army Co-operation pilots—53 men who were given a six-day conversion course before being sent into action. By sunset on 18 August, new Hurricane and Spitfire pilots joining operational squadrons were so green that few had flown ten hours

solo on either type of aircraft. Of the 2365 pilots who fought in the Battle of Britain, 446 died. When addressing the House of Commons, Winston Churchill made his famous statement: 'Never in the field of human conflict has so much been owed by so many to so few.'

Goering's next orders called for round the clock bombing of British targets. Thus, on 24 August began a series of attacks with the intention of making the invasion of Britain feasible. After four raids on that day, Manston was temporarily abandoned. In fact, Manston and Lympne, both on the Kent coast, were on several occasions in-

Far right Perhaps overshadowed by today's powerful supersonic machines, these Battle of Britain Hurricane IICs still look full of fight

operable: even Biggin Hill was so damaged that for one week only a single fighter squadron could use this important sector station. Fortunately, at the critical moment, Hitler himself stepped in and switched the weight of the attack from airfields to London.

By 1 September, invasion barges were to be seen in increasing numbers in and near Ostend; and numbers of larger vessels began to build up at Dunkirk, Calais and Flushing. A further ominous sign was the setting up of a long-range artillery battery at Cape Griz Nez.

Coastal forces were alerted and a few German spies were caught after landing on the South East coast. Their orders were to monitor troop movements in the Home Counties. Invasion seemed imminent, and the signal went out to Britain's defence forces—'Cromwell': it was the code word for immediate action.

At last the defenders get it right

The 7-15 September launching of the Luftwaffe blitz on the capital brought to a head the most controversial issue of the Battle of Britain. When Hitler turned on London in daylight, the forward defences were swamped and some 300 bombers and 600 fighters of the morning raid were little molested until East London dockland was ablaze and the raiders on their way home. Only then had a competitive force assembled, including No. 1 (RCAF) Squadron of Spitfires, Nos 303 and 310, two Polish squadrons of Hurricanes and two additional RAF squadrons, No. 19 (Spitfires) and No. 242 (Hurricanes). The Luftwaffe was harassed homewards losing at least 40 aircraft to 28 defensive RAF fighters.

And so to the day which in retrospect spelt the beginning of the end for Germany in World War 2: 15 September 1940. It was

This Spitfire has dived very close to the German He111 bomber from which the photograph was taken. The proximity made the air-gunner's aim very difficult, but enabled a deflection shot possible as the fighter pulled away. The pilot's right manoeuvre would have been to make a hard bank and climb away to spoil the German's aim

the day Dowding, Park, Trafford, Leigh-Mallory, and their ground controllers, the pilots and the machines finally got it right. The setting was pure theatre, it was almost as if a script had been provided right down to the detail of Churchill appearing with his wife at Park's No. 11 Group Operations Room at Uxbridge, Middlesex. As if on cue, Park told the Prime Minister: 'I don't know whether anything will happen today'—and then it did!

Given exceptional radar warning because of the time taken by the Luftwaffe to assemble 250 bombers and 700 fighters across the Channel, Park was able to anticipate the enemy force with 11 of his 21 squadrons in the air. He had ten squadrons in five sets of pairs, while from No. 10 Group to the west No. 609 Squadron's Spitfires were racing to cover the Vickers factory at Weybridge, Surrey.

Bader's Big Wing succeeds

Behind London, a 'Big Wing' of 60 Hurricanes and Spitfires of No. 12 Group was also assembling, led by Squadron Leader Douglas Bader, the legless pilot. Forward, Park's paired squadrons, Hurricanes to engage the bombers and close fighter escort, Spitfires to divert the high-flying screen of Me109s, did well. But Bader's Big Wing gave the Luftwaffe the greatest shock it had yet encountered, fighting with an aggressive spirit en-gendered by its leader. The weapons of the few now drove the Luftwaffe in headlong retreat from London.

Hurricane and Spitfire pilots were elated at the results of fighting in larger formations following frustrating weeks of confronting major raids in threes, sixes or at best nines and twelves. Fourteen Hurricane squadrons made Central London the graveyard of any raider that got through. Although history does not date the end of the Battle of Britain until 31 October, the Luftwaffe's daylight loss on 15 September of some 60 aircraft to the defenders' 26 (respective contemporary claims were 175 and 53) was enough to dissuade Hitler from invasion.

He began reluctantly to consider postponing the invasion from mid-September on. Signs that this was true were noted on 20 September, when warships began moving from the Channel ports and the thickly packed invasion barges were disappearing. Again, that invaluable source Enigma finally convinced Britain that the invasion had either been postponed or abandoned when specialist admin units, set up for the invasion, were disbanded.

On 22 June, 1941, 120 German divisions attacked Russia with 3200 tanks. Operation Barbarossa had begun. And 7,000,000 Germans, 500,000 German allies and 21,000,000 Russians were to die before the last member of the Wehrmacht was thrown back from Russian soil.

Below The wreckage of one of two FW190s shot down over England's South Coast. This aircraft was reported to have been brought down by Bren-gun fire aimed by an Army sergeant

1941

As 1941 ended, with London being bombed by the Luftwaffe time and time again, culminating in the incendiary + HE bombs raid of 29 December, when 30,000 fire bombs dropped on to the City area to leave St Paul's Cathedral isolated in a sea of flames and destruction, it was the time for Britain to hold fast. The threatened invasion by Germany had been first postponed and then cancelled due to the valiant efforts of the pilots of the RAF's Hurricanes and Spitfires in seeing off the bombers of the German Air Force and forcing Goering to embark upon a night offensive against Britain's cities and their civilian populations. Throughout 1940, shipping losses had continued at a frightening rate notwithstanding the welcome victory over the pocket-battleship *Graf Spee* the previous December. But still, 1000 merchantmen and most of their crews had been sunk for the loss of 22 U-boats.

On land, Hitler was planning his attack on his recent ally Russia, even while the ink on their non-aggression Pact, signed in August 1939, was barely dry.

The early days of 1941 saw Cardiff laid waste on the night of 2 January; then Bristol received the same treatment the following night. The population of Britain, bloody but unbowed, looked for some small sign of encouragement—any sign so long as it gave hope for the future.

To survive, Britain had to get her supplies through in the convoys: the alternative was plain, that or be starved into submission, it was that simple. In some way the menace of the U-boats had to be defeated or at the very least their success rate had to be drastically cut. The war in the Atlantic was a bitter, unrelenting struggle fought without mercy. Our convoy routes were known to German Naval Intelligence and wolf-packs of U-boats would lie in wait across the known headings of the groups of plodding merchantmen.

Then, on 20 May, a German paratroop drop of 5060 men, some in gliders, landed on the isle of Crete. Greece had been invaded by Italian forces, their Duce, Benito Mussolini, hoping to impress Hitler and to prove that his army was an effective fighting force. Crete, still in Allied hands up to then, had been occupied by British and Commonwealth troops as a means of defence. They also posed a threat to the Axis since Crete could be used as a stepping stone to the mainland of Europe. So the island had to be taken, but taken quickly.

The German blitzkrieg eastwards through Russia and towards Moscow—always the goal of Hitler's territorial ambitions—was in full swing. On 11 July, the Panzers were approaching Smolensk, and beyond that city lay Moscow. Marshal Timoshenko's soldiers were given the task of holding off the Germans and did so until 5 August. It was, on the face of it, just another German victory, but the battle's length and severity drained the impetus of the Panzers and gave the Soviets time to strengthen their defences round Moscow. The consequence was that Germany would in time suffer the fate of every other invader trying to conquer the immense tracts of Russia, its weather and its seemingly inexhaustible supply of manpower. The Russian defence of Smolensk was a major battle of World War 2 and finds a place in this chapter because it was yet another hammer blow to the German threat of European domination.

The attack on Pearl Harbor is never described as a Battle. President Roosevelt called it a 'day of infamy', for on 7 December, while Japan's naval air forces were striking at the unprepared warships at anchor along Battleship Row in Pearl, her diplomats were still 'negotiating' in Washington. However, while the damage to the US Fleet was devastating the effect of the attack was to rebound on the Axis. The sleeping giant of the US military machine, backed by an incredible arms industry, would rise and put America alongside the Allies.

Merchantships are easy prey to submarine attack. Huge sinkings were experienced by such ships in September 1939. During the summer of 1940 British convoys had been suffering crippling losses in the North Atlantic. The U-boat commanders had discovered that asdic was ineffectual against surfaced submarines. Detection depended upon the human eye with the doubtful aid of starshell at night.

From their position low down on the water, surface ships were visible even on a dark night, at a considerable distance, silhouetted against the sky. Communications between escorts were primitive, the radio telephone (RT) was not only unreliable but working on high frequency (HF) could not be used for plain language messages. So searchlight was the main form of communication and this, of course, only in daylight. The advantage was on the side of the U-boats in locating convoys and they were able to de-code the British naval cipher, giving them the routes of individual convoys. The first U-boat to sight the convoy would radio the fact to HQ, who would organize a concentration of submarines which would gather on the surface ahead of the convoy and close in to attack after dark.

'To make destruction easier'

Moving slowly on the surface, the U-boats would pass undetected between the widely separated escorts, selecting their targets from the columns of ships. The most skilful of them, Otto Kretschmer, captain of *U99*, had initiated the practice of penetrating between the columns to make destruction easier and discovery by the escorts more difficult.

About 30 U-boats were operational in 1940, but by the spring of 1941 100 were in commission and available to Admiral Erich Doenitz, head of Germany's U-boat arm. Up to then, escorts for convoys had been gathered at random, often old sloops or *Flower*-class corvettes. Both types were slow; they were equipped with asdic and depth-charges.

Captain Donald Macintyre, commanding the escort force, describes the action that followed in his own words:

"At the beginning of March 1941, I had orders to take command of *Walker* and one of the new escort groups being formed. The idea was that such groups were to be kept together.

I had met none of my subordinate captains when I led 5th Escort Group to sea a few

Atlantic convoys were mostly long periods of boredom as the slow-moving columns of ships ploughed steadily across the sea. But when a U-boat struck there would be sudden and frantic action, especially if the ships were ordered to scatter. Captain Macintyre (inset) commanded the escort group for Convoy HX112 and tells his story in this chapter

days later. The group was unusually strong, with, besides *Walker*, four old destroyers, *Vanoc*, *Volunteer*, *Sardonyx* and *Scimitar*, and two corvettes *Bluebell* and *Hydrangea*. At that time, outward-bound convoys were escorted to about 18 degrees west longitude. The escorts then moved off to intercept a homeward-bound convoy.

South of Iceland, where we were to meet Convoy HX112, Doenitz's three most successful U-boat commanders were waiting, part of a wolf-pack.

The three—Gunther Prien, of *U47*, who had sunk the battleship *Royal Oak* in Scapa Flow, Joachim Schepke, *U100*, and Otto Kretschmer of *U99*, were rivals in the race to be the first to sink 300,000 tons of Allied shipping. Kretschmer was in the lead with 282,000 tons.

But the careers of this deadly trio were about to come to an end. Prien had already gone to a watery death with his entire crew, being hunted to destruction by the destroyer *Wolverine*, the end coming in a tremendous explosion and a vivid red flash from under the water.

U-boats converge on HX112

That day passed quietly for convoy HX112 and its escort, but the British radio listening posts stations had detected a unit signalling an enemy report to U-boat HQ. We were being shadowed: soon the U-boat pack would be converging to attack. The night

Below The purple-outlined asdic beam from a corvette searching for a U-boat. But it is on the surface and the wave-pattern combined with the small surface-area of the submarine breaks up the reflected signal, making detection impossible

Bottom A rendezvous in the Atlantic between two U-boats of the Mk VII class. Both Kretschmer and Schepke commanded submarines of this kind during their attack on Convoy HX112

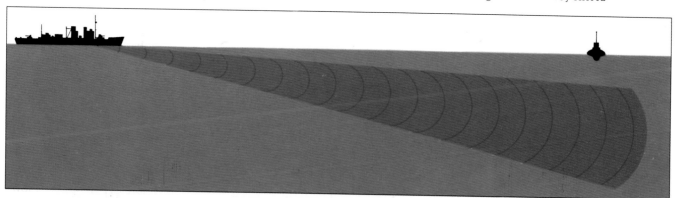

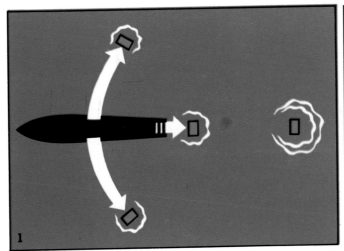

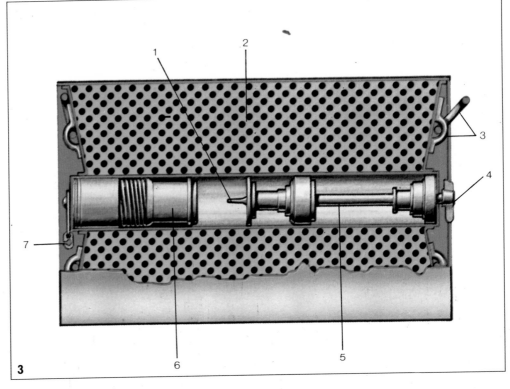

1 A destrcyer could throw patterns of depth-charges from the sides as well as dropping them off the stern. This enabled a large area of sea to be covered during an attack upon a submarine

2 The U-boat hunters' usual plan was to drop depth-charges in such a way that they fell round a diving U-boat. The pressure from all sides when the charges exploded would then tend to crush the submarine's shell and destroy her

3 Mk VIII Depth Charge
Ejected by Thorneycroft 'Thrower' firing 1 kg (2 lb) charge.
1 Detonator
2 Explosive charge, cordite
3 Lifting lugs
4 Depth setting key
5 Pistol
6 Primer and primer placer
7 Safety clip

had closed down and was dark and moonless but showing a clear-cut horizon dividing the calm sea and a starlit sky—ideal for a sub attack from the surface.

The report had come from Lieutenant Commander Lemp, of *U30*. In answer to his call, *U100*, *U99*, *U74* and *U37* took a course which would intercept the convoy. Not waiting, on the night of 15 March, Lemp moved in towards HX112's starboard-wing column. He fired two box torpedoes, then turned away and fired a stern tube. It was a hit and the petrol-tanker *Erodona* burst into flames.

Meanwhile, expecting further attacks, the escorts kept to their screening positions, on every bridge anxious eyes strained to

pierce the darkness. We were lucky in that, out of the converging wolf-pack, *U74* never managed to find us; while *U37* got in the path of a large tanker when in a fog-patch and received such damage that she was forced to limp back to base.

But we were up against two U-boats worth a whole wolf-pack of less deadly raiders. Both made contact during 16 March and shadowed us from the edge of the horizon. Kretschmer kept out of sight, but late in the afternoon the over-confident Schepke came too close and was sighted by *Scimitar*. Excited at the prospect of some real action I swept out at high speed with *Scimitar* and *Vanoc*. At the estimated position where the sub had dived we began a systematic sonar

search for it. But the U-boat evaded us.

So long as the U-boat was kept down, the convoy was getting away from the danger zone. Leaving the other two escorts to continue the hunt for two hours I took *Walker* back to rejoin the convoy. The first of Kretschmer's victims, another petrol-tanker, blew up at 2200. During the next hour, five more ships were torpedoed, all but one of which went to the bottom, leaving lifeboats and rafts with survivors dotting the surface of the sea.

How could the darkness be penetrated and the attackers destroyed? Our one hope was to sight a U-boat's tell-tale wake, give chase to force her to dive, and allow the asdics a chance to bring depth-charges into action. I put *Walker* into a gently curving course, thereby covering every point of the compass under a penetrating probe. And it worked!

The U-boat crash-dives

As *Walker*'s bows swung, a thin line of white water came into the lens of my glasses. I shouted orders, increasing speed to 30 kts and altered course towards the target. The U-boat spotted us and crash-dived in a cloud of spray. A swirl of water lingered as we passed over the area and sent a pattern of ten depth-charges crashing down.

It was not possible to miss. The depth-charges detonated with great cracking explosions and huge waterspouts rose to

Top The veteran destroyer *Walker*, which attacked *U99* and depth-charged the vessel to the surface

Above HMS *Vanoc* photographed off Norway before she was modified for anti-submarine duty

Top *Hydrangea*, typical of the two *Flower*-class corvettes that were part of the Fifth Escort Group

Above Also in the Fifth Escort Group was HMS *Scimitar*. She saw *U100* before *Vanoc* fatally rammed and sunk the U-boat

Inset Schepke, who was crushed to death when *Vanoc* rammed his U-boat

Right Kretschmer walks ashore to captivity. His torpedoes had sunk 282,000 tons of Allied merchant shipping

masthead height astern. Then another explosion followed and an orange flash momentarily spread across the surface. We thought that it was our first 'kill'—but I had not learned how hard it was to kill a U-boat. our depth-charges had exploded too deep to do fatal damage. And when our sonar detected the submerged target there began a long duel with *U100*, in which *Vanoc* was called to join in.

Taking it in turns to run in to the attack, pattern after pattern of depth-charges went down as we tried to get one to within the lethal range—about 6 m (20 ft)—of our target. But Schepke managed to escape destruction, though heavily damaged.

We pulled away to rescue survivors and allow the severely disturbed water to settle down. If we left the area, the U-boat commander might think he had shaken us off and be tempted into some indiscretion. So we picked up the master and 37 of the crew of the *J. B. White*.

'Have rammed and sunk U-boat!'

We had hardly got under way once more when I saw that *Vanoc* was going ahead at full speed. Then she signalled: 'Have rammed and sunk U-boat.' Our losses in the convoy had been partly avenged. Schepke had surfaced to chase the convoy and *Vanoc* had seen the wake. *U100* went to the bottom with most of her crew, including Schepke. I circled *Vanoc* as she picked up the few survivors.

Then *Walker's* sonar reported he was in

contact with yet another sub and I took *Walker* into the attack. Then all the instruments broke down at the crucial moment, so Lieutenant John Langdon timed his attack using very primitive methods, then gave the order to fire. As the charges exploded we ran on to get searoom for further attacks: but as we turned there came the thrilling signal from *Vanoc*: 'U-boat surfaced astern of me.'

Vanoc's searchlight beam settled on the sub. Both destroyers opened fire, but it did not matter. The U-boat signalled she was sinking and the crew were in the water as she plunged to the bottom. We picked them up and under the watchful eye of a sentry, Germany's foremost U-boat ace dropped into an exhausted sleep in my cabin.

With grim satisfaction I ordered the Germans on deck as we steamed through the convoy the next morning. Standing on the quarter-deck with *Walker's* Chief Engineer, George Osborne, Kretschmer commented on the coincidence of our horseshoe crest and his being similar, but on his U-boat the points were downwards. 'Well, you let the luck run out that way,' grinned the Chief, bringing a rueful laugh from the prisoner."

For the first time, radar had been instrumental in a U-boat sinking—an indication of the turning of the tide in the dual between U-boats and escorts. The whole Atlantic became the 'battlefield' with convoys escorted by warships and aircraft throughout the crossing. Both sides had heavy losses until the battle of the Atlantic was won by the Allies in 1943.

THE FALL OF CRETE

The battle for Crete is unique as the first massed paratroop drop in the history of war. It was a battle lost by 'kindness' by the British and won by bluff and determination by the Germans. But it could easily have been their first major defeat on land in the war. What led to the aerial invasion of Crete? In October 1940 Italy invaded Greece from Albania. When Hitler decided to attack Russia he realized that he must secure his right flank, for the Rumanian oilfields at Ploesti could be reached by bombers from Greece or the Greek islands. So Germany intervened in the Greek campaign and by the beginning of May 1941 she held the Greek mainland. Only Crete remained.

On 20 April 1941 plans were submitted for an airborne attack by paratroops of the 7th Airborne Division. The German transport was the tri-motored Ju52. It was a rugged aircraft with a range of 1280 km (800 miles).

The German 7th Air Division had details

of the garrison on Crete—as at December 1940: 5000 men, 400 at Heraklion and the rest in and around Canea; 30 tanks, 30 anti-aircraft (AA) guns, 40 AA machine-guns, two heavy coastal guns and 300 vehicles.

But in 1941 the garrison consisted of 28,000 British and ANZAC troops with Greek and Cretan irregulars—a total strength of 42,500. Many of the men from the 6th Australian and 2nd New Zealand Divisions were veterans of the Greek campaign who had been evacuated to the island.

When Major-General Bernard Freyberg, VC, arrived to take command he had only three weeks to familiarize himself. He found that battalions had been placed to cover the airfields at Maleme, Retimo and Heraklion, the capital Canea and the important harbour and docks at Suda Bay. The garrison was spread across the coastal plain covering a variety of potential landing areas.

The Germans laboured with their usual energy to prepare for attack. Weapons containers from France, stored in preparation for the invasion of Britain, were delivered. Fuel, nearly 3 million litres (650,000 gallons), was obtained. Logistics problems were solved. The first wave of paratroops left early on 20 May, and the second wave took off soon after. It was a chilly morning. At about 0700 the Luftwaffe arrived to make their usual morning raid.

Far left Three weeks before the invasion of Crete the docks area of Suda Bay was bombed by the Luftwaffe

Left This *unterfeldwebel* ('under-sergeant') of paratroops is armed with pistol, stick-grenade and 9 mm Schmeisser MP40 submachine-gun

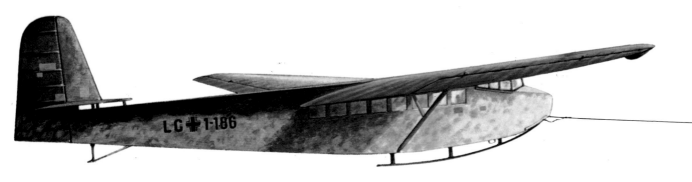

Above A DFS 230B-1 German glider is towed by the sturdy old Ju52. Over Crete 493 of these aircraft were employed in ten transport groups

Thirty minutes later there were new attacks. To the defenders, it seemed that a continuous stream of planes was above the island. At Maleme, the airfield was attacked by Ju88s and ground-strafed by Me109s, and the Bofors guns on the airstrip fired until only one remained.

The gliders came hissing down

At 0800 the attack ended and an 'eerie silence' fell. Then the gliders came hissing down carrying men of the 1st Battalion of the Assault Regiment. Their job at Maleme was to neutralize the AA guns and take Point 107, which dominated the airfield.

Elsewhere, gliders landed in Prison Valley near Canea and by the heavy AA guns on the Akrotiri Peninsula. For many of the Germans this was their last journey, ending in a bullet-shredded fuselage crumpled against a rocky hillside. The pilots had been told the valley was a plateau, but it was strewn with boulders.

Before the last glider had bounced to a halt the paratroopers began to jump from the Ju52s. Caught under fire in midair, they were picked off easily. Even after landing the survivors remained vulnerable. Some carried MP38 SMGs, many were armed only with Luger pistols, but neither 9 mm weapon had much of a range. Until they reached the containers for their heavy weapons the paratroopers could be picked off by riflefire.

Most of the Germans who survived were bunched in small defensive groups, but

Below Map of the airborne assault on Crete

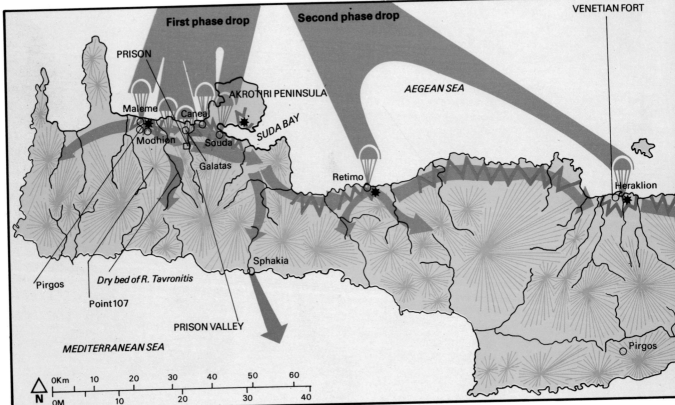

GERMAN DFS 230B-1 GLIDER IN TOW BY JU52

they soon began to join up into effective forces. Paratroopers who had dropped west of Maleme airstrip and glider troops who landed around the Tavronitis bridge had had time to assemble in Prison Valley. Their dropping zone was unmolested, but they were trapped there.

At German HQ, reports from Crete were few. General Kurt Student now put the second phase of the operation into action. Maleme may have been bad and the landings round Canea unsatisfactory but the attacks which followed at Retimo and Heraklion were worse.

The 2nd/1st and the 2nd/11th Australian Battalions were dug in at Retimo, on the hills that overlooked the road and airstrip. On the afternoon of 20 May they reduced a force of 1500 paratroopers to 1000 men, broken into disorganized groups. The Aussies held the strip and the Germans who managed to attack Retimo had to fight quite unexpected opposition from armed Greek gendarmerie.

Heraklion was held by Australian and British troops. The preliminary bombing did not keep their heads down, for some units had arrived after the German attacks. Heavy fire greeted the paratroopers as they started to jump. The Black Watch were ready and concentrated their fire as each stick of men left the aircraft. The German plan had gone awry. Instead of a massed drop, lone Ju52s were coming in and releasing their paratroopers right over the defenders.

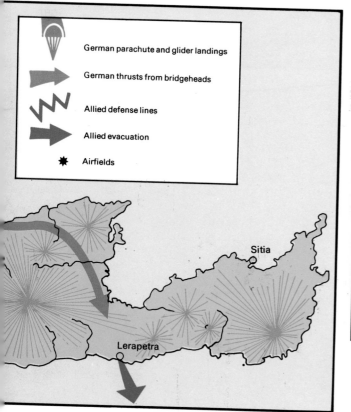

German parachute and glider landings

German thrusts from bridgeheads

Allied defense lines

Allied evacuation

★ Airfields

Sitia

Lerapetra

Below Mountain troops of the German 5th Division board a Ju52 to be taken directly to Maleme airfield, the first and most important objective of the assault

Above A German paratrooper has located his ammunition box, dropped separately. Often they fell far away

Above A German paratrooper sees follow-up sticks coming down

Right This German PAK 36 AT gun is well-sited to pick off an enemy moving along the main street in Retimo

Bottled-up in a Venetian port

The men who dropped to the west of Heraklion made their way towards the town and found themselves caught in heavy fighting with British and Australian troops. With Greek help, the Allies pushed most of the Germans out of the town and bottled them up in the Venetian fort by the docks.

By the afternoon of 20 May, Student was in radio contact with his men in Prison Valley. He learned that they were trapped and could not break out. It was night when he heard of the failure of the Heraklion attack; there was silence from Retimo. So far the Allies were winning. They knew that they should counter-attack while the Germans were weak, but were convinced that a seaborne assault was imminent. They did not know that almost all the paratroops had been committed.

Student now knew what was going on, but the New Zealanders in the area were out of touch. Lieutenant Colonel W. L. Andrew, VC, knew that not only was his battalion out on a limb, exhausted and under-strength, but believed it would be attacked by superior air and ground forces the next morning. He decided to pull back.

But the enemy had gone!

The next morning the tired Germans made their way up the hill, but their enemy had gone. Then the Germans' Captain Kleye landed on the edge of the airstrip, sent by Student to get an update on the situation. His Ju52 landed without being fired on. By 0800 six supply aircraft had touched down and Student decided to reinforce his unlikely success. At 0900 two parachute companies were dropped west of the Tavronitis. A supporting drop east of Pirgos landed near the New Zealand 5th Brigade but suffered heavy casualties.

More JU52s roared in with cargoes of men and equipment. Maleme was still under fire from the garrison, and damaged aircraft began to block the runway, so the Germans used POWs to clear the wreckage away.

That night the Allies watched as searchlights and gunfire lit up the sea to the north. The German 'invasion fleet' had been sent out unprotected by the Luftwaffe. It was located by radar and intercepted. For two and a half hours the Navy's Force D attacked, thinking that they had killed a large number of Germans, but many were rescued. Only 309 were dead and many had escaped to nearby islands. Another convey turned back before being located.

Freyberg allocated two New Zealand battalions, 1500 men, for an attack on Maleme. They had a long march to the airfield. In the dark they met the survivors of the German 3rd Battalion and at Pirgos men of the supporting 21 May drop. This held the New Zealanders up and it was dawn by the time they reached Maleme—too late. The skies were now held by the Luftwaffe, so the attack was called off.

Student had committed himself to Maleme. His troops at Retimo and Heraklion were to hang on and contain the garrison. The 5th Mountain Division went into the hills to outflank the New Zealanders, planning to take Canea and open up Prison Valley to release the Paratroopers trapped there.

Freyberg now knew that he could not hold

Below Having grouped into a fighting unit, paratroops charge into action

Bottom The end is in sight for the defenders as German supply columns are landed. This one is on a road near Suda Bay

the island. Men who thought they were winning were shocked to learn that they were being evacuated. By 25 May the Germans were close to Canea. They attacked the village and forced out its defenders. But that evening it was the turn of the Germans to fight a desperate defensive battle.

Blood-curdling battle-cries

A counter-attack was pressed home against the Germans with blood-curdling battle-cries. In savage hand-to-hand fighting the Germans were ejected from the village. But Student had landed at Maleme and by the 27th paratroops had captured Canea. British and New Zealand forces began a withdrawal to the port of Sphakia, where commandos had been landed, and although they were not trained for the role they fought a skilled withdrawing action covering the garrison.

On 28 May the Navy lifted all the men from Heraklion. At Retimo the survivors of the 2nd Parachute Regiment were trapped and attacked. Though many Australians were captured, about 700 Germans were killed.

At Sphakia, men sheltered in caves and waited to be taken off. During the operation the Navy lost the AA cruiser *Calcutta* and destroyers *Hereward* and *Imperial*. But the greatest loss was the cruiser *Orion*. Bombed, she sank and 260 men lost their lives.

By the end of May the Navy had evacuated 18,000 men, but 5000 were left behind. In all the British and Commonwealth troops lost 1742 killed and 11,737 wounded, with 11,835 POWs, out of 42,500. The Royal Navy lost nine warships, with 127 damaged and the RAF had 465 aircraft destroyed.

The Germans won the battle for Crete, but it was costly. Out of 22,000 men, they suffered 6000 casualties, 1990 dead and 1955 missing. Of the 493 transports, 220 were destroyed. The greatest casualty was Hitler's confidence. Two months after the operation he said: 'The day of the parachutist is over. It is a surprise weapon and without this element there can be no future for airborne forces.'

Paratroops were never used on critical targets such as Malta or Cyprus, where they could have affected the course of the war.

German troops mopping up British soldiers who thought that they had beaten the aerial invasion. But the victory cost the German Army dear, it suffered 6000 casualties in the action

THE BATTLE FOR SMOLENSK

Before they could stage a Moscow-bound offensive, the Germans had first to secure the Smolensk land-bridge. For armour, this was the shortest and easiest route to Moscow. To the north lay the forests and swamps of the Upper Berezino river; to the south, the Pripet marshes, where tanks were useless.

To spearhead the drive east, vanguards of the German Fourth Army were *Panzergruppen 2* and *3*. Following were Second and Ninth infantry armies to secure and occupy the ground won by the Panzers.

On 1 July, Fourth Army had to break through towards Moscow, cross the Dnieper, then spearhead due east to seize the Yelnya Heights over the river Desna. *Panzergruppe 3* was to swing north-east round the Berezino marshlands and dash

160 km (100 miles) east to the plains round Smolensk.

The Russians knew the importance of this landbridge. Indeed, the Soviet High Command intended to contain the German advance long enough to build a defensive line before Moscow. The Smolensk counter-offensive was led by Marshal Semyon Timoshenko.

The Soviet reserves at Vyazma consisted of nine infantry divisions. At Bryansk there were another 12. Their artillery was horse-drawn, except for the medium guns, which were pulled by tractors. Of the two tank brigades, the 104th and 106th, only the latter was equipped with the new T34.

The German offensive opened on 3 July with a thrust towards Polotsk. They got to the eastern bank of the Dvina, but two Soviet

A battle map of the bitter assault on Smolensk. The massive resources of the Red Army were not strong enough to stem the German tide

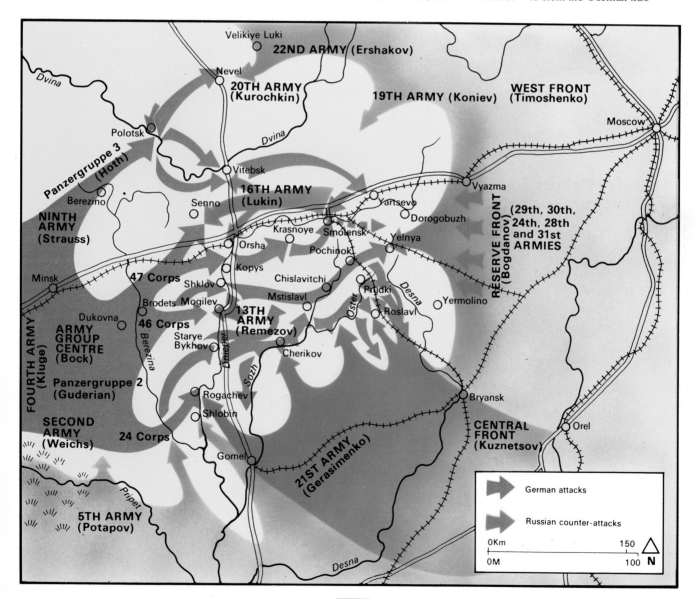

SOVIET AIR FORCE POLIKARPOV 1-16

Above The Soviet Air Force's Polikarpov 1-16 fighter

Below Marshall Semyon Timoshenko, commander of the Russian counter-attack at Smolensk

Bottom right German infantry fight their way through the suburbs of Smolensk

tank brigades momentarily held them up.

Farther south, the Germans advanced in three columns. The northern one, 47 Panzer Corps, struck out from the Dneiper just below Orsha on their way to Dukovna. The centre column, 46 Panzer Corps, closed in on Magilev. In the extreme south, 24 Panzer Corps headed up the Oster valley. The next day, 24 Panzer Corps reached the Dneiper near Rogachev, establishing a bridgehead on the opposite bank.

Thirty kilometres (20 miles) behind, other German units crossing the Berezino were attacked by Soviet 5th Army, holed up in the Pripet marshes, but the Russians concentrated their strength along the Dneiper. at Brodets, 15 km (10 miles) south of Berezino, *SS Das Reich Division* ran into heavy resistance, but managed to push on. Here, the Russians blew the Yakchizy bridge up, but German engineers worked round the clock and had it ready for heavy vehicles on 5 July.

The Russians were massing for a counter-attack south of Rogachev at Shlobin. On 6 July, they crossed the Dneiper and fell on 24 Panzer Corps' right flank. The Soviet drive was checked by 10 Motorized Division, which occupied Shlobin. The Germans guessed that the Russians were going to make a stand on the river. Then they heard that 17th Panzer Division had been halted near Senno in a fierce battle. It marked the end of Army Group Centre's blitzkrieg in Russia. German HQ was worried. Fourth Army had gone far enough. But they had to keep up the pressure on the trapped Soviet units in the Minsk pocket and wait for the Second and Ninth Armies to catch up. The Soviet build-up on the Dneiper was obviously aimed at cutting off the Panzer threat.

But Guderian wanted to forestall the Soviet counter-drive by striking rapidly across the Dneiper and hurling the Russians off balance.

German Fourth Army is exhausted

Which action was right? Both and neither. There was too much emphasis on the defeated Soviet remnants in the Minsk pocket and Pripet marshes. On the other hand, the main Russian threat was on the Dneiper. But the German Fourth Army was exhausted after its dash across eastern Europe.

Nevertheless, Guderian planned to strike across the Dneiper. On 7 July, *Panzergruppen 2* and *3* mopped up the Russians in their sector and resumed the north-east advance towards Polotsk. In the south, the Soviets strengthened the garrisons at Rogachev, Orsha and Mogilev, and moved to blunt 17th Panzer Division at Senno.

During the battle, 17th Panzer tried to pin the Russians down. The new target for 47 and 24 Panzer Corps was Starye Bykhov, starting 10 July. The next day, 46 Panzer Corps would cross the Dneiper at Shklov

and 47 Panzer Corps would cross at Kopys. Meanwhile, Timoshenko's HQ was on Guderian's south-west flank. He planned a counter-attack across the Dneiper.

Weather halts the Wehrmacht

Summer thunderstorms had hindered the Germans in the north, the roads turning into a morass. The Panzers were frequently forced to halt, but despite this some Soviets inside Polotsk were trapped. The Germans entered Vitebsk on 9 July. With it in German hands, the northern flank of the landbridge was secured.

On 10 July, *Panzergruppen 2* and *3* crossed the Dneiper without difficulty, but 10th Panzer Division, spearheading 46 Corps, came under air attack in Shklov.

Above Troops of the Soviet 20th Division being told of the latest situation before Smolensk. By now, most of the 20th Army was trapped

Left The formidable Russian T34/76A, an AFV which established Red superiority over the German tanks. It had a 76 mm gun and two or three MGs

T34/76A (WELDED TURRET MODEL)

mained, trapped to the east of the town.

The significant German breakthrough was in the north, where they crossed the Dvina on either side of Vitebsk on 13 July. But Soviet 116th Army then attacked Yartsevo, capturing it on 15 July.

Meanwhile, the Russians opened their counter-offensive in the south, striking north-west from Gomel and aimed at the rear of the German right flank. But the Russians were forced to commit their precious reserves here instead of at Starye Bykhov as originally intended.

Now, *Panzergruppe 2* rushed towards Smolensk, but the city had been abandoned a few days earlier. Smolensk was entered on 16 July, where 300,000 Russians were trapped. The Germans were now looking towards the next probable Soviet defensive line, the Yelnya Heights. Break that and the road to Moscow was open. The 3rd and 4th Panzer Divisions were grappling with the Red 21st Army along the west bank of the Oster.

The period 18-20 July can be called the pivotal point of the Smolensk campaign. Russian HQ committed 400 new T34 armoured fighting vehicles (AFVs) in the Smolensk area, where the trapped Soviets made many attempts to break out. The Germans were determined to prevent this. On 23 July five Red divisions managed to get away along the Dneiper valley.

Now, 18 fresh Soviet divisions were deployed between Yelnya and Cherikov. On 24 July the Russians attacked, with heavy artillery in support, 10th Panzer losing a

Above German troops about to break into a Russian cottage. Little mercy was shown to the unfortunate civilians in this brutal period

Below German Pioneers use a flame-thrower to flush out a Russian bunker. The defenders were usually asphyxiated as all the oxygen was consumed by the flames

Soviet artillery was effective here, and much better than the Germans.'

Between Orsha and Mogilev two German salients bulged ominously eastwards: *SS Das Reich* secured a bridgehead in Shklov and thrust east. South of town, 10th Panzer and the *Gross Deutschland* Infantry Regiment did likewise. And south of Mogilev, 3rd Panzer tried to surround the town while 4th Panzer struck east towards the Minsk-Moscow highway.

In Mogilev, Soviet 13th Army tried to evade 3rd Panzer Division, met *Gross Deutschland* and battled for four days. The Germans began to run out of ammunition on 13 July, so they slackened fire. Now, only six divisions of the Red 13th Army re-

third of their AFVs but holding firm. Some 50 Russian tanks were destroyed.

Red Army's horrifying losses

In effect, the Germans had been forced to fritter away their army in a local battle not even part of the original invasion concept, Barbarossa, the invasion plan, was now permanently upset.

All Russian resistance ended in the Smolensk pocket on 2 August. Just in time,

for the Germans were down to half their tanks. Russian losses were terrifying, losing 310,000 prisoners, 3205 AFVs and 3210 guns. The Russians had bought time, at terrible cost, but the Germans were too exhausted to push on to Moscow. Smolensk must be viewed as a great German tactical victory but an overall strategic defeat. The conquest of Russia, Hitler was beginning to realize, was unattainable—like the invasion of Britain a year before.

Above A Soviet gun crew in action, about to load the 6 kg (14 lb) shell into the breech of their 76 mm gun. It could reach nearly 10 km (7 miles)

'KATYUSHA' BM13 ROCKET LAUNCHER

Left The famous Katyusha rocket launcher. With a crew of six, it fired 16 132 mm rockets. The model illustrated is probably a post-war version

Far right A Zero works down a line of US Army P40s on Wheeler Field, Oahu, in the film 'Tora-Tora-Tora!'

Ford Island as seen by the Japanese pilots as they made their punishing attack on Pearl Harbor. The huge oil dump seen in the right-hand background somehow remained untouched. Its loss would have been disastrous to the US Fleet

Japan's strike at Pearl Harbor on 7 December 1941 is often presented as a surprise attack on the US Navy, yet relations between the two countries were so strained it was inevitable that for Japan to get her expansionist ways in Asia she would have to use force against the US.

But US naval strategists did not think an attack on Pearl Harbor at all likely. According to them, such an action would be impressive but yielding Japan no great benefits.

When the strike was proposed by Admiral Isoruku Yamamoto in September 1941 the idea was rejected. Its lack of any military value apart, an attack on Pearl Harbor would snap the already strained relations between the two countries and all-out war would result.

So Yamamoto bypassed his High Command and approached Emperor Hirohito's brother, Prince Takamatsu, then a navy staff officer based in Tokyo. He was intrigued and told his brother, who bypassed military advisers and gave the go-ahead.

In October 1941 the US was warned of a planned strike against Pearl by an unusual source. Richard Sorge, Moscow's master spy in Tokyo, passed the information to the Russian dictator Joseph Stalin, who in turn told Washington. But American naval strategists still considered an attack unlikely.

Japan the 'peacemaker'

On 5 November Japan decided to make one more diplomatic approach to Washington before unleashing the now fully rehearsed attack. It was not intended to succeed, merely to give Japan the veneer of 'peacemaker'.

The force destined for the attack left Japan almost a fortnight before the 29th. It was powerful—six aircraft carriers and nine destroyers with tankers and supply ships, two cruisers and two battleships in support. Twenty ocean-going submarines acted as an advance guard. Five of these were equipped with two-man midget subs.

By 6 December, American experts were still saying an attack was most unlikely. Their grounds for such confidence were the belief that Japan was launching a full-scale amphibious operation in the south and Japanese ships laden with soldiers were reputedly entering the Gulf of Siam. Surely Japan would not mount two naval operations at the same time.

As dawn rose on 7 December, the Japanese carrier force had reached a position 440 km (275 miles) north of Pearl. Fifty-one Aichi 'Val' dive-bombers, 43 Mitsubishi Zero-Sens 'Zeke' fighters, 40 Nakajima B5N2 'Kate' bombers with shallow-running torpedoes and 50 high-level 'Kates' left the decks at 0600. Eighty Vals, 54 Kates and 36 Zeros followed up.

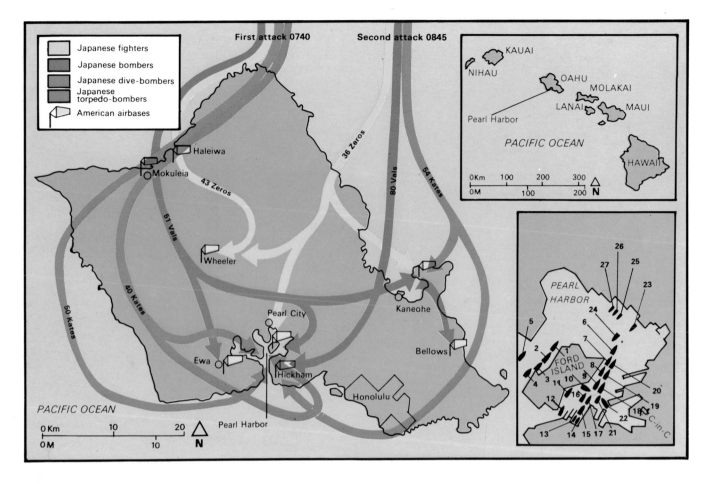

Above The main map shows the approach of the first and
second waves of the Japanese attack of Pearl Harbor.
Inset, bottom, gives the positions of the US Pacific Fleet at anchor

USS *TENNESSEE* (1943)

USS *Tennessee* escaped more
lightly from the Japanese
attack than some of the other
US battleships. Along with
Maryland, she was moored in
'Battleship Row'. Both were
protected on the seaward
side by *Oklahoma* and *West
Virginia*. This meant that
Tennessee escaped being
torpedoed. But she did suffer
two bomb hits. The first struck
the centre gun of turret 2,
cracking the barrel and
putting all three guns in the
turret out of action. The
second smashed through the
roof of turret 3, damaging the
structure and the rammer of
the left gun

The US warships lying at anchor at Pearl kept a 'Condition 3' state of preparedness. Every fourth gun was supposed to be manned but the ammunition for the machine-guns was in locked boxes. The keys were in the charge of officers, some not even on duty.

A bosun's mate saw between 20 and 25 aircraft approaching at 0730 but could not identify them. The first bomb dropped just before 0800. Naval air commander Rear-Admiral Bellinger broadcast the words that were to smash the isolationist grip on the US: 'Air Raid, Pearl Harbor! This is no drill!'

Blunders and bad luck

The US Pacific Fleet was caught with its pants well and truly down. Blunders and bad luck brought about this American debacle. One certain blunder was when two NCOs, manning a radar station, saw Japanese planes closing in and watched them for 40 minutes. They tried to raise the

Above Destruction on an airfield on Ford Island after the attack. In the background the USS *Arizona* explodes after breaking in two

After modernization, *Tennessee* was active in the Pacific in World War 2, seeing action off Tarawa, the Marshalls, New Ireland, the Marianas, Palau and Leyte Gulf. **Laid down** 14 May 1917; **Launched** 30 April 1919; **Length** 190.3 m (624 ft 6 in). **Beam** 29.5 m (97 ft 3 in); (34.5 m (114 ft) from 1943); **Displacement** 33,000 tons (40,500 tons from 1954); **Complement** 57 officers, 1026 men in 1920 (90 officers, 2219 men from 1943); **Armament** 12×14 in, 16×5 in, 40×40 mm, 43×20 mm; Equipped with two aircraft in 1943 (one catapult); **Speed** 21 kts

alarm, but nobody believed them! The USS *Ward* gave another warning at 0645 when she sank a midget submarine at the mouth of Pearl Harbor. This too was ignored.

Commander Mitsuo Fuchida was in charge of the first wave. At 0755 the bombs began to fall. Their target was Battleship Row—eight battleships at the south-east of Ford Island—and four were holed or damaged in five minutes. While the Kates punished the vessels below the waterline, Vals were smashing decks, bridges and gun-turrets. Other Kates were finishing off the job with high-level bombing. The initial attack inflicted shattering losses on the Pacific Fleet. USS *Arizona* blew up and snapped in two. More than 1000 men were drowned. Three torpedoes smashed into *Oklahoma*. She turned over, imprisoning her crew below decks. When holes were cut in her bottom only 32 survivors crawled out. Four torpedoes and a bomb sunk the *West Virginia*, while the *California* blazed for three days after fires reached her fuel tanks. Then she sank.

USS *Nevada* tried to steam out of the harbour but Japanese bombers caught her and she finally beached at the harbour entrance. *Maryland* and *Tennessee* escaped relatively lightly. They were shielded from torpedoes by *Oklahoma* and *West Virginia*, which were moored on the seaward side. The flagship of the US Pacific Fleet, *Pennsylvania*, was in drydock and was more or less unscathed. Japanese pilots expended valuable torpedoes on the old battleship *Utah*, in use as a target ship for some time.

At the north-western shore, Japanese aircraft damaged the light cruiser *Helena* and the seaplane tender *Curtiss*, while the light cruiser *Raleigh* was crippled. The minelayer *Ogala* was sunk. The destroyers *Shaw*, *Cassin* and *Downes*, the light cruiser *Honolulu* and the repairship *Vestal* all suffered damage.

While the fleet in the harbour was being pulverized, the airfields on the mainland were also taking a battering. At the US Marine Corps' Ewa Field 49 airworthy planes were hit, leaving only 16 intact. Kaneohe was a flying-boat base for Catalinas—27 were write-offs and six severely damaged. It was one of the most punishing attacks on airbases in World War 2. Of the 148 first-line naval aircraft, at least 112 were destroyed, as were 52 out of the 129 Army planes. Thirty-eight American planes took off, ten were shot down.

The first Japanese wave departed. Its attack had lasted 25 minutes. In that time thousands of American lives had been lost and millions of dollars worth of strategic

weaponry destroyed. There was more to come.

At 0845, 36 Zekes, 54 torpedo Kates and 80 high-level Kates provided Japan's second wave. But now the Americans were more prepared. Shore batteries opened up and a few still-serviceable ships' guns. Japan lost only nine planes in the first wave. In the second, the score rose to 20, in return for little effect. The fuel depot escaped, and it held as much oil as Japan had in her entire reserves.

'Day that shall live in infamy'

President Franklin D. Roosevelt spoke of the 'day that shall live in infamy'. If it was it was also a day of appalling military cost to the US. The Japanese had lost 29 aircraft and 55 men. For this meagre expenditure 2403 soldiers, sailors, airmen and civilians had been killed, 164 planes destroyed and six battleships and three destroyers sunk, while a number of others had been severely damaged. Apart from the dead, the Japanese left 1178 wounded Americans at Pearl. Had the Japanese sent in a third wave, there is no doubt that Pearl could have been totally devastated.

But the isolationist grip on America was smashed, she was now at war with Japan. The attack on Pearl, while brilliantly successful, unleashed the might of the US military machine against Japan, Germany and Italy. For Japan the end would come when she was totally demoralized and Hiroshima and Nagasaki had been razed by the first atom bombs.

Left One of the most obvious warnings of hostile Japanese action was this midget submarine, spotted at the mouth of Pearl Harbor before the attack

Below Why did the US Navy C-in-C at Pearl ignore all the warnings? Centre is Admiral Husband E Kimmel

Left Wrecked destroyers *Cassin* and *Downes* in what was a dry dock before the attack. Behind them is the USS *Pennsylvania*, Pacific Fleet flagship. At right background is the light cruiser *Helena*. Two stunned navy personnel stand at the head of the dry dock, wondering how all that shattered equipment is going to be salvaged and repaired

1942

It was described as the greatest commando raid ever staged, and it prevented the huge German warship *Tirpitz* from berthing in the largest dry dock in the world, from whence it could emerge to menace Britain's merchant-shipping life line. The dock was built at St Nazaire, on the Biscay coast of Occupied France. Afterwards, the threat of more large-scale raids kept considerable numbers of German soldiers on the alert, forces which could have been far more effectively used on the horrendous Russian front. How the raid succeeded and brought hope to the oppressed French is the opening battle in this chapter.

The Japanese, having hit the US below the belt at Pearl Harbor, were well on the move and the Rising Sun was making its brutal presence felt in the Pacific. But in the fragmented area between Alaska and the eastern seaboard of Russia there is a chain of islands called the Aleutians. For the Japanese, they would be a perfect stepping stone between East and West—and vice versa. In late May 1942 a Japanese Carrier Strike Force headed north to reach the Aleutians by 3 June. There followed a confused struggle between the invaders and the US Army for possession of this remote area. It was fought in Arctic terrain and in Arctic weather and its outcome is also one of this chapter's battles.

In Europe, Cologne was battered unmercifully by 1000 RAF heavy bombers on the night of 30 May. Called dramatically Operation Millenium, it devastated 600 acres of the ancient city, killed nearly 500 people and made 660,000 survivors homeless. Now, over 40 years later, the mass raid seems cruel, but to the citizens of Britain's cities it was no more than just retribution for the unceasing Luftwaffe raids on their towns and cities.

By July 1942 the war in North Africa had ebbed and flowed, with General Erwin Rommel's Afrika Corps waging a brilliant tactical campaign, striking east towards a hitherto unheard-of place called El Alamein. Then in three days the all-conquering Afrika Corps was stopped in its tracks by the British Eighth Army, an important battle, critical for the outcome of the Desert War. Auchinlech had transformed a rout into a victory by sheer powers of leadership.

Had not this first battle of Alamein been won by the British Eighth Army, the better-known and much more publicised second battle of Alamein fought by General Montgomery over 12 days in the following October-November might never have been contested and the desert war would have been protracted.

The next battle in this chapter takes us back to the war-torn Pacific and the yellow tide of Japanese Imperialism sweeping through those idyllic island chains. Between the Solomons and the New Hebrides lies the Santa Cruz group. It is here that a bloody battle was fought between the US South Pacific force and Japan's Combined Fleet. It was a battle with no outright victor, but at the end Yamamoto's aircraft had been reduced by 100 and the death toll was high enough to prevent Guadalcanal from staying in Japanese hands.

The North African desert was the setting for the last battle in this chapter. By mid-1942 each side both Allied and Axis knew that they could win—or lose—the war. Now was the time, then, to blood the new GIs in a land battle, for the air and naval forces had already had plenty of combat experience and had proved themselves. The arena was the large naval base at Oran. It had to be wrested from its defenders, the Vichy French, Zouaves, Algerians and those tough French Foreign Legionnaires. The battle was confused, as so many are, sometimes bordering on tactical disaster, due to lack of tripartite communication between the three services. But it showed that the GI could learn from experience and prove his mettle as a fighting man. All this was to be invaluable when the time came to enter Europe in 1944. The story of the taking of Oran concludes this chapter.

ST NAZAIRE

Admiral Karl Doenitz, Commander-in-Chief of Germany's submarine forces, asked a U-boat commander what he would do if the British mounted a raid on this strategic Atlantic port. The arrogant, complacent reply was that emergency plans had been prepared. Doenitz said: 'I shouldn't be too sure.' In fact, the raiders were already on their way.

St Nazaire held the key to a potential death stroke. It contained the only dry dock on its stretch of the coast and the only one large enough and deep enough to accommodate Germany's most formidable battleship, the 42,900-ton *Tirpitz*.

She had eight 15 in guns, other formidable armament, and could outpace all her British rivals. Using the St Nazaire dock, being let loose in the Atlantic, her effect, combined with the U-boats, could well be fatal to the Allied convoys.

The idea of denying the dock to the *Tirpitz* had already been mooted. It was futile to try to destroy the lock gates from the air. Precision bombing against AA defences at St Nazaire was out of the question, and less discriminate, high-level bombing involved the town and French civilians. And in 1942 the RAF had no bomb that could destroy those monster caissons. Built of steel, each was 50.9 m (167 ft) long, 16.5 m (54 ft) high

and 10.5 m (35 ft) thick, and contained compartments filled with water to enable them to cope with the huge pressures involved in flooding or emptying the dock. Sabotage was unlikely to work, the place was too heavily guarded.

The port seemed impregnable

St Nazaire seemed impregnable. Fortunately this idea did not last for long. Vice-Admiral Lord Louis Mountbatten's imagination was fired by the concept of the raid. Maps, aerial photographs, drawings of the dock (originally built for the SS *Normandie*), charts showing defences, even a table-sized model of the objective, all were already in existence.

It was obvious that transport for the raid could not be left to small craft. So many Commandos were needed to carry out the demolition work that a large ship was necessary. The choice was an old destroyer, HMS *Campbeltown*. But she was not to serve simply as a troop transport. She had an additional—and suicidal—purpose. The destroyer, carrying just over four tons of TNT fitted with delay fuses, was to ram the caisson of the lock gates. Then she would be scuttled. Eight hours after ramming the fuses would detonate, blowing up the ship and caisson. In case she failed to ram, the

Above Ten months after the raid—an aerial photograph shows that the dock area is still in a state of chaos

Below HMS *Campbeltown* wedged fast in the dock gates after her valiant attack. In her bows are 24 depth-charges and 4 tons of TNT all of which exploded two days later, when her decks were crowded with German naval and military personnel

Above German troops move past fallen British commandos. The raid was successful, but at cruel loss of life

Right The job of *MTB74*, seen in a West Coast harbour, was to torpedo the dock should the Campbeltown fail to get there and ram it

Opposite page, top inset shows the routes taken by the raiding force to and from St Nazaire. The main map gives the approach to the dock. In the lower inset, a plan of the St Nazaire dockyard showing the objectives of the MGB and MTB

job of destroying the dock was to be done by *MTB74*, which carried delayed-action torpedoes.

Campbeltown's complement of 80 Commandos would deal with secondary targets, assisted by other troops carried in 16 MLs and a gunboat, *MGB314*. The commandos were also to capture and hold the southern lock lifting bridge, along the eastern side of the basin, so that there would be an escape route to the waiting launches.

Campbeltown arrived for conversion at Devonport on 10 March. Within 15 days she had been transformed to resemble a *Mowe*-class torpedo boat. Eight 40 mm Oerlikons replaced the original 4 in guns. Four rows of 6 mm (¼ in) armour plating were fitted to the

deck. The bridge was surrounded by more armour-plate, so the captain, Lieutenant Commander Samuel Beattie, could steer the ship. The four-ton explosive charge was put in a tank placed abaft the pillar that supported the forward turret. On ramming the gates, *Campbeltown*'s bows would crumple up to, but not beyond, this pillar.

The venture, code-name Operation Chariot, was blanketed in secrecy. But German suspicions were roused by the peculiar behaviour of 60 RAF bombers which appeared over the docks at 2330 on 27 March. The pilots were to drop only one bomb per run, keep above 1830 m (6000 ft) and not attack targets other than the dock and the Penhouet Basin. The Germans were

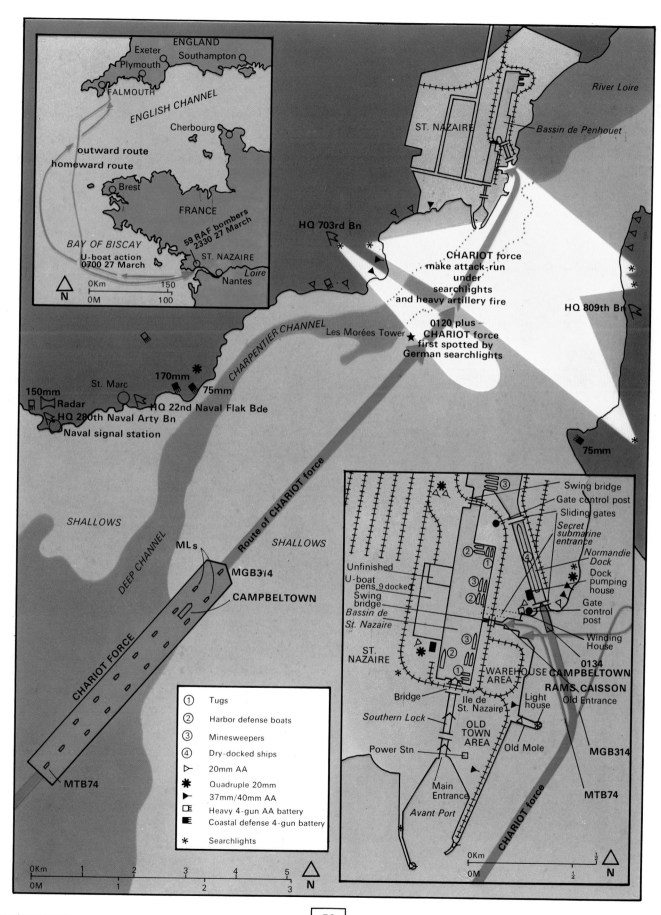

ENGLAND

Exeter
Plymouth
Southampton

FALMOUTH

ENGLISH CHANNEL

Cherbourg

outward route
homeward route

Brest

FRANCE

59 RAF bombers
2330 27 March

BAY OF BISCAY

U-boat action
0700 27 March

ST. NAZAIRE

Loire
Nantes

0Km   150
0M   100

N

ST. NAZAIRE

River Loire

Bassin de Penhouet

HQ 703rd Bn

CHARIOT force
make attack-run
under
searchlights
and heavy artillery fire

HQ 809th Bn

0120 plus –
CHARIOT force
first spotted by
German searchlights

Les Morées Tower

CHARPENTIER CHANNEL

170mm

75mm

150mm

St. Marc

Radar

HQ 22nd Naval Flak Bde

HQ 280th Naval Arty Bn

Naval signal station

75mm

SHALLOWS

MLs

SHALLOWS

Route of CHARIOT force

DEEP CHANNEL

MGB314

CAMPBELTOWN

CHARIOT FORCE

MTB74

Swing bridge
Gate control post
Sliding gates

Secret
submarine
entrance

Normandie
Dock

Dock
pumping
house

Gate
control
post

Winding
House

Unfinished
U-boat
pens 9 docked

Swing
bridge

Bassin de
St. Nazaire

ST.
NAZAIRE

WAREHOUSE
AREA

0134
CAMPBELTOWN

RAMS CAISSON

Bridge

Ile de
St. Nazaire

Light
house

MGB314

Southern Lock

OLD
TOWN
AREA

Old Mole

MTB74

Power Stn

CHARIOT force

Main
Entrance

Avant Port

① Tugs
② Harbor defense boats
③ Minesweepers
④ Dry-docked ships
▷ 20mm AA
✳ Quadruple 20mm
▶ 37mm/40mm AA
▭ Heavy 4-gun AA battery
▬ Coastal defense 4-gun battery
∗ Searchlights

0Km   1   2   3   4   5
0M   1   2   3
N

0Km   ½
0M   ¼
N

Right Two German members of a U-boat crew stand on the prow of their submarine as it approaches the pens at St Nazaire

thoroughly alerted by this timely warning.

The raiders were some 13 km (8 miles) away, near the Le Chatelier shoal. *Campbeltown* was towing her understudy, *MTB74* and the force was escorted by two destroyers, *Atherstone* and *Tynedale*. *Campbeltown* lightly scraped bottom at 0045 on 28 March and again ten minutes later. Apart from this all went smoothly until shortly after they had passed the Les Morees tower at 0120, when they were about 2 km (1¼ miles) from the dock.

'According to orders'

Suddenly a searchlight stabbed out. Two 20 mm gun bursts gave a warning and signal lamps winked. A signalman on *Campbeltown* earned a four-minute reprieve by flashing back a message explaining that they were making for St Nazaire 'according to orders'. But a recognition signal in the wrong shade of red gave the game away.

Searchlights bathed the Channel in blinding light. At 0128 the German shore guns opened up. *Campbeltown* took most of the punishment. Shells tore her hull, her fo'c'sle was set ablaze and badly holed and a direct hit on the foredeck destroyed a 12-pounder and some mortars. The mortar crews were all killed, as were many Commandos lying close-packed on the deck. British guns pounded back at the

Below HMS *Campbeltown* (formerly USS *Buchanan*, supplied by the US under the Lend-Lease arrangements) shown before and after her conversion for the St Nazaire raid. The conversion was begun at Devonport on 10 March 1942, and was completed in 15 days

Germans to such effect that after three or four minutes the enemy guns faltered.

At that moment *Campbeltown*, at 20 kts, was bathed in tracer, heading on course for the lock gates. In the glare of searchlights, Beattie took *Campbeltown* surging on, her Oerlikons at full blast. She tore through the anti-torpedo nets and at 0134 smashed into the caisson, 10 m (35 ft) of her bows buckling like tinfoil. Her captain could not have done better. The explosive charge inside the ship was just 1.5 m (5 ft) from the lock gate.

HMS *CAMPBELTOWN* (BEFORE CONVERSION)

HMS *CAMPBELTOWN* (AFTER CONVERSION)

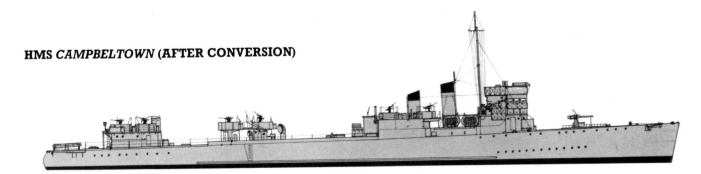

Now, German resistance was ferocious. Half the men aboard *Campbeltown* were killed or wounded, and only 40 per cent of the remaining troops could get ashore. All fought bloody battles to achieve their objectives. Many succeeded, but at fearful cost.

A group got ashore, sprinted through heavy 20 mm fire, drove Germans to flight and put explosives in their guns. Under intense German fire, Captain William Pritchard's men lowered their HE charges into the boiler-rooms of two tugs, then more explosives under a bridge. Pritchard was bayoneted to death, his enemy himself shot by British machine gun fire.

Lieutenant Stuart Chant had been lacerated by shrapnel on board *Campbeltown* but had orders to wreck the dock's pumping machinery. He blew the steel door off, charged down the stairs 12 m (40 ft) below ground and laid his charges. Great blocks of concrete flew through the air when the HE exploded, the floor of the pumping house collapsed and the control machinery became a pile of debris.

The winding house of the dock was also wrecked, and at the inner caisson explosives were planted and twelve 8 kg (18 lb) charges were suspended on the Penhouet side. The officer in charge, Lieutenant Robert Burtenshaw, was killed after storming a German tanker inside the dock. His Sergeant, Frank Carr, blew the explosives and water flooded through the damaged gate into the dock.

What was left of the landing parties made their way towards the Old Entrance. But the motor launches to take them off had been destroyed, wreckage and floating bodies littered the water.

The entire dock area rocked

Of the naval personnel, 34 officers and 157 ratings were killed or missing; 59 military personnel were killed or missing, 109 returned home and another 109 were taken prisoner. One of these was Lieutenant Commander Samuel Beattie. On 29 March, Beattie was being questioned by German Intelligence men. Just after 1000 *Campbeltown*'s charges exploded, the entire dock area rocked. About 300 German officers and men were aboard *Campbeltown* at the time, and as the ship's forward half disintegrated, the after-section was carried into the dock where it sank. The dock was useless and never used by the *Tirpitz* or any other heavy German ship.

The Nazaire raid, perhaps the greatest Commando raid ever, produced a psychological spin-off, for the Germans became obsessed by possible further raids of that magnitude. A disproportionate number of troops were kept to man the French coastal defences, diluting the Wehrmacht elsewhere, and Britain's merchant shipping had had a major threat removed.

Above The officer in charge of the naval phase of the raid on St Nazaire, Commander R. E. D. Ryder

Below British commandos and seamen are marched into captivity by German soldiers after the fighting had stopped

A chain of extinct and active volcanoes, shrouded in fog and mist, fringed with reefs through which fierce currents of warm and cold water swirl—the Aleutians stretch 1600 km (1000 miles) from near Alaska to the International Date Line. Add 80 kt gales, and a mean annual temperature of 38°F (3.3°C), and some idea of the conditions found in this bleak area can be imagined.

So in World War 2 nature prohibited any westward offensive through the Aleutians, even though Brigadier General William Mitchell said: 'If Japan seizes Alaska she can take New York.' The Japanese knew the area, having carried out many pre-war exercises in northern waters, themselves thinking that US bombers could reach the Japanese islands from the Aleutians.

On 5 May 1942 Japanese Imperial HQ ordered a carrier strike on Dutch Harbour, while an assault force occupied Attu, Kiska and Adak. So on 24-25 May 2nd Carrier Striking force, two heavy cruisers, three destroyers, the light carriers *Ryujo* and *Junyo*, left Japan heading east. Two Occupation forces totalling 2450 men, headed for the islands. This Northern Area Task Force was led by the cruiser *Nachi*. Submarines and seaplanes were recon-

noitering Kiska, Amnchitka, Dutch Harbour and Kodiak.

Aware of the Japanese movements, the US and Canadian forces in the Alaskan area organized a surface search by US Coast Guard cutters, backed by B17s, Liberators, Catalinas and seaplanes. A strike force of nine destroyers, plus 109 fighters and 47 bombers was deployed for defence and anti-shipping strikes. Rear Admiral Robert Theobald was patrolling to the south with five cruisers and four destroyers.

The Japanese force flew off 23 bombers and 12 fighters on 3 June, striking Dutch Harbour 290 km (180 miles) north-east. Next morning, 26 more planes hit Dutch Harbour, destroying 11 US aircraft, killing 43 GIs and causing damage to a hospital wing, oil tanks and a hangar. The Japanese lost 11 planes shot down by P40s from Otter Point, an airfield unknown to them.

A week of confusion

In the following confused week the Japanese occupied Attu with 1200 men, taking 39 civilian prisoners. Kiska weather station was seized by 1250 men of special Landing Force No. 3 and 700 troops. When the US discovered the occupation of Attu,

In the bitter cold Aleutian weather a US 60 mm mortar team load their weapon during the fighting on the Chichagof Ridge on Attu. For both sides the weather was probably their worst enemy, grounding aircraft and making life in general very uncomfortable

USSR

BERING STRAIT

ARCTIC CIRCLE

Fairbanks CANADA

Kiska Occupation Force (Ohno) sailed 26-27 May

BERING SEA

KOMANDORSKIS

KISKA

SEA OF OKHOTSK

ALASKA
Anchorage

ALASKAN HIGHWAY

KODIAK

Dawson Creek

Sitka

USA

ALEUTIAN ISLANDS

ATTU
AGATTU

Paramushiro

ADAK
AMCHITKA

US battleships (Pye)

Vladivostok

Attu-Adak
Occupation
Force (Omon)
sailed
27-28 May

US
N. Pacific
Force (Theobald)

JAPAN

1st Carrier
Striking
Force (Nagumo)

2nd Carrier Striking Force
(Kakuta) sailed 24-25 May

San Francisco

Main Body (Yamamoto)

Midway Invasion Force
Main Body (Kondo)
Transport Group (Tanaka)

MIDWAY

PACIFIC OCEAN

US Carrier Striking Force (Fletcher)

HAWAII

WAKE

SAIPAN
GUAM

Minesweeper
Group
(Miyamoto)

INTERNATIONAL DATE-LINE

0Km   1000   2000   3000

N

0M   1000   2000

Top The Japanese submarine
I26 which reconnoitred the
Aleutians on 25 May 1942

Above In July 1943 the US fleet
bombarded Kiska in an effort
to soften Japanese resistance
to US invasion

Left Map shows the location of
the Aleutian Islands between
Alaska and the Japanese
bases in the Kuriles, Guam,
Saipan and Japan herself.
Indicated are the dates of
sailings and routes of the
Japanese task forces and the
positions of the opposing fleets

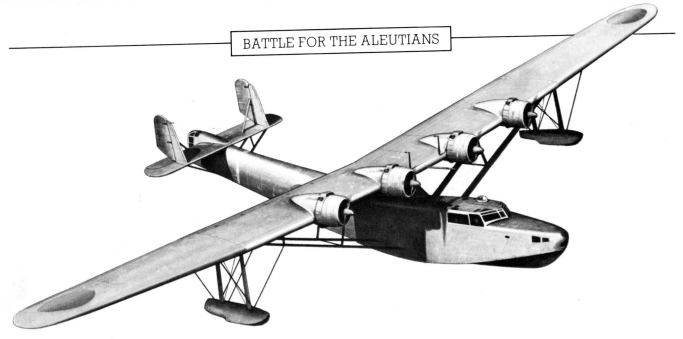

KAWANISHI H6KS 'MAVIS' JAPANESE FLYING-BOAT

air raids were launched by Catalinas. They did some damage but the threat of retaliation forced their withdrawal and the evacuation of 62 Aleuts from Atka. Submarines, aircraft and surface ships were used to try to cut the Japanese supply lines and to prevent any further advance through the islands.

By now neither the US nor the Japanese were sure which islands were occupied by the enemy during the rest of 1942. On 7 August five cruisers and four destroyers approach Kiska and in a 30-minute bombardment barracks, barges and flyingboats were wrecked; then the *Kano Maru* was set

ablaze and later destroyed by Catalinas.

With no Japanese on Adak, the US built an airfield there on 30 August. B24s, P38s and P39s raided Kiska on September 14 and ten days later wrecked transports, seaplanes and installations. On 16 October, B26s sank the destroyer *Oboroto* 50 km (30 miles) north-east of Kiska and damaged the *Hatsuharu*, while on the 26th *S31* torpedoed the Japanese merchantman *Keizan Maru* anchored at Paramushiro.

The high-speed minesweeper *Wasmuth* broke her back when two depthcharges fell overboard during a gale on 29 December, and the 11th Air Force lost 63 aircraft due to

Below A USN Catalina flies low over one of the Aleutians on a reconnaissance mission. The very inhospitable terrain, coupled with terrible weather, made military operations difficult

bad weather, compared with only nine lost in action.

The campaign moved into 1943 as a cruiser and destroyers bombarded Attu, Chichagof Harbour and Holtz Bay on 18 February. Attempts to reinforce Attu were made by the Japanese commander Vice Admiral Kawase, but they failed. The US made sure when 100 warships and 200 aircraft bombed and shelled the 2630 Japanese there.

Japanese suicide charge fails

Then on 11 May 11,000 men of the US 1st Division landed north-west of Holtz Bay. The GI combat boots were not up to the terrain or cold, but despite it, and in face of fierce opposition from the defenders, the Americans pushed on. By 29 May 1000 Japanese were penned in mountains between Chichagof Harbour and Sarana

Bay. They made a suicide charge against the GIs and fought until the last killed themselves with hand-grenades. The capture of Attu cost the US Army 600 dead and 1200 wounded. Using the airfield, the US dropped 1255 tons of bombs on Kiska in ten weeks. In the end they did not even reply with AA fire.

Americans and Canadians started going ashore on Kiska on 15 August, when 29,126 GIs and 5300 Canadians landed. The enemy did not react, except for a few shadowy figures in the ever-present mist. But they were American, 25 were killed and 31 wounded by their own side.

The 6000 Japanese had left on 28 July, two weeks before the Allied invasion. The Aleutian campaign was costly, untidy and wasteful, but it was the end of any threat to invade North America through those islands.

Left The Mavis flying-boat. **Wingspan** 40 m (131 ft 2¾ in); **Length** 25.5 m (84 ft 1 in); **Height** 6.3 m (20 ft 6¾ in); **Wing area** 169.4 sq m (1829.86 sq ft); **Engines** 4 × 1300hp Mitsubishi Kinsei 53 14-cylinder radial air-cooled; **Armament** 20 mm cannon in tail turret, two 1764 lb, four 1100 lb or 550 lb, or 12 132 lb bombs or two 1764 lb torpedoes, 4 × 7.7 mm MGs mounted in forward and aft dorsal turrets and beam blisters; **Crew** nine; **Top speed** 385 k/h (239 mph) at 5940 m (19,685 ft); **Cruising speed** 253 k/h (161 mph) at 4000 m (13,120 ft); **Service ceiling** 9550 m (31,365 ft); **Normal range** 4941 km (3070 miles); **Maximum range** 6775 km (4210 miles)

Left A stick of American bombs on its way down to a Japanese troop camp. There are already bomb craters on the ground

Below The progress of the Aleutian campaign. It was vital for the US to dislodge the Japanese from the area because of the threat to Alaska and, eventually, the American and Canadian States below

Occupation 7.6.1942
BERING SEA
Holtz Bay
Landings 11.5.1943
Carrier plane strikes 3-4.6.1942
Chichagof Harbor
ATTU/SHEMYA
AGATTU
Occupation 15.8.1943,
Occupation 12.1.1943
Dutch Harbor
Occupation 7.6.1943.
Makushin Bay
TANAGA
UNIMAK
KISKA
ADAK
Otter Point
UNALASKA
Occupation 30.8.1942
UMNAK
B17 base
Occupation 7.6.1942.
AMCHITKA
ATKA
KANAGALSI
Landings cancelled 6.6.1942

ALASKA
Anchorage
Kodiak
COOK INLET
KODIAK
GULF OF ALASKA
Fort Randall
Cold Bay

Japanese forces
US forces

0Km 150 300
N 0M 100 200

Far right The first three days of the First Battle of Alamein were critical. This map shows the attack and counter-attack situation of the opposing forces

It has been said about the war in the desert that before Alamein we never had a victory, after Alamein we never had a defeat. It could have been said with greater justice of General Sir Claude Eyre Auchinleck's more protracted battle at Alamein lasting almost four weeks in the preceding July.

Auchinleck had dismissed General Neil Ritchie and assumed command on 25 June. Eighth Army had lost 50,000 men in the past month. The British Cavalry, who provided most of the armour, partly owing to sheer military ignorance and to ineptness, had lost face with the rest of the army, especially ANZAC and South African units.

High morale of the Afrika Corps

In contrast, the morale of General Rommel's Afrika Corps was high. They had no thought but that of destroying the British forces and eventually controlling the Central and Eastern Mediterranean, finally taking the Suez Canal. But Rommel's forces were small. His 15th and 21st Panzer Divisions and 90th Light Division had only about 60 serviceable tanks and 2500 men. The Italian armoured and motorized divisions had about 44 tanks and 2500 infantry.

Yet British Intelligence gave the Germans 25,000 men and 100 AFVs. There were 183 German and 238 Italian operational aircraft, a total of 421 as opposed to 463 in the Desert Air Force. All Rommel's victories had been won by exceeding his safety limits and chancing his arm. But this time he would be facing Auchinleck—the 'Auk'.

In the Mersa Matruh position the British still had about 150 AFVs, including 50 American Grants, three weak infantry divisions and the 2nd New Zealand Division. Numerically, they had more tanks and infantry than the Germans and about the

Wearing typical Afrika Corps clothing, a Wehrmacht sidecar team ploughs through soft sand on a recce. There was little protection if attacked, so mobility was the key factor

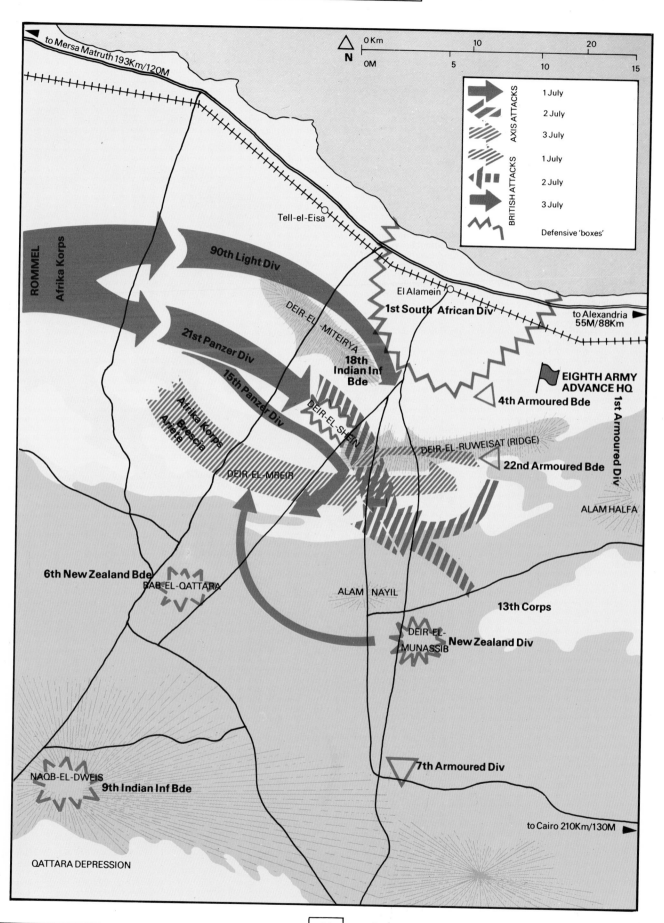

N

0 Km ... 10 ... 20
0M ... 5 ... 10 ... 15

AXIS ATTACKS
1 July
2 July
3 July

BRITISH ATTACKS
1 July
2 July
3 July

Defensive 'boxes'

to Mersa Matruth 193Km/120M

ROMMEL Afrika Korps

90th Light Div

21st Panzer Div

15th Panzer Div

Afrika Korps
Brescia
Ariete

DEIR-EL-MREIR

Tell-el-Eisa

DEIR-EL-MITEIRYA

El Alamein

1st South African Div

to Alexandria 55M/88Km

18th Indian Inf Bde

DEIR-EL-SHEN

EIGHTH ARMY ADVANCE HQ

4th Armoured Bde

DEIR-EL-RUWEISAT (RIDGE)

22nd Armoured Bde

1st Armoured Div

ALAM HALFA

6th New Zealand Bde

BAB-EL-QATTARA

ALAM NAYIL

13th Corps

DEIR-EL-MUNASSIB

New Zealand Div

NAQB-EL-DWEIS

9th Indian Inf Bde

7th Armoured Div

to Cairo 210Km/130M

QATTARA DEPRESSION

Above A British Crusader tank Mk II, with its puny 2 pdr gun. A movie cameraman is perched on the turret

same number of aircraft. On the right, holding the Matruh defences was 10th Corps. First Armoured Division lay to the south, with 7th Armoured, now reduced to light forces.

The 'Auk' had arrived just in time. Rommel attacked on 26 June, aiming to crash through a gap, then swing to the south to envelop 13th Corps. He hoped to entice the British into committing their tanks into battle independently. The next day all was confusion. The RAF were forced to abandon six fighter airstrips and fall back towards the Delta. Many opportunities were lost to punish Rommel's rash penetration. Even 10th Corps had to fight its way out, losing 7000 troops and 40 tanks. The Germans had now reached Fuka, 95 km (60 miles) from Alamein. The New Zealanders shook themselves free in a hand-to-hand battle by moonlight, then charged across the German

Right German armoured vehicles are unloaded at Tripoli and destined to boost Rommel's forces

Far right British POWs resting beside a captured armoured car which the Germans have fitted with a 28 mm PAK AT gun alongside the standard Vickers MG

6 PDR MK II

Left Six-pounder Mk II AT gun at part traverse. **Calibre** 57 mm; **Weight** 1.2 tons; **Crew** 4; **Penetration** 80 mm at 457 m (500 yd); **M/velocity** 2935 km/h (2675 fps)

camp in their vehicles. The battle had degenerated into a confused withdrawal to the 'last ditch' at Alamein.

The Alamein position was just a line stretching 60 km (38 miles) across the desert from the soft sand and salt marshes of the Qattara Depression to the coast near El Alamein.

Three defended 'boxes' about 25 km (15 miles) apart were constructed: the first and strongest at El Alamein, wired and mined by the 1st South African Division; the second 11 km (7 miles) to the south at Deir-el-Shein having 23 25-pounders, 16 6-pounder AA guns and nine Matilda AFVs; the third box at Bab-el-Qattara was occupied by 9th Indian Infantry Brigade. Behind this screen Auchinleck was reorganizing his army.

Late on 30 June, 3000 infantry of 1st South African Division faced Rommel, with most of the 50th British and 10th Indian Divisions which had got away from Matruh. Auchinleck intended the boxed garrisons to canalize the German advance, the mobile forces would attack his flanks and rear.

GRANT MK I

All artillery was put under Eighth Army command to centralize its firepower. Like Rommel's *Panzerarmee* guns and the British armour was strictly ordered to fight 'close-hauled' within range of friendly artillery support.

The German 90th Light Division and the two Italian armoured divisions were already exhausted, having had no rest from action for five weeks, and their numbers were shrinking. On 30 June, when Rommel reached the Alamein position he had only 55 tanks. He knew that if he gave the British a chance the advantage would lay with them.

Rommel's reconnaissance was faulty
Rommel did not hesitate. As at Matruh, he would smash through the position, swing

Below The Grant Mk I medium tank (Lend Lease US M3) which equipped 8th Army from early 1942. **Weight** 28.5 tons; **Crew** 6; **Guns** 75 mm (sponson) 37 mm (turret); **Armour** 13-57 mm; **Speed** 42 k/h (26 mph)

Right British armoured cars under attack from Stuka dive-bombers and getting very near misses

Above A Bren-gun carrier crew of the 9th Rifle Brigade keep watch on a burning supply dump

Below A three-ton lorry is hit and thick smoke fills the air as its precious cargo of fuel burns

north to the sea, penetrate the gap and then swing south to round up whatever British forces were left. H-hour was fixed for 0300 on 1 July. But his reconnaissance was faulty, he did not know of the box at Deir-el-Shein at the west end of Ruweisat Ridge. Then as the evening advanced he found that his Afrika Corps would be late. He should have waited a little longer and made sure where the British were.

Just before 0900, 15th Panzer found that 18th Indian Brigade was holding Dein-el-Shein. Two-thirds of them had never been in action and were short of ammunition, but they were in no mood to give in when called to surrender. A full-blooded attack by 21st Panzer lasted six hours before 2000 defenders were captured. Then 22nd Armoured Brigade's tanks sent to their relief clashed with part of 15th Panzer and drove them west.

The German 90th Light, caught in concentrated converging fire of the South African artillery, were forced to dig in and at the end of the day there were only 37 German tanks left out of 55. Undaunted, Rommel decided to resume the attack on 2 July, but the 90th Light again failed to make headway, so he called off the planned sweep and tried to cut the coast road.

Eighth Army hits back

Auchinleck decided now to hit back, using 13th Corps attacking westwards, 1st Armoured Division and the rest of the Corps striking north. Both British and German attacks started almost simultaneously and a confused action resulted. Rommel was now down to 26 tanks. One more push, he thought, might break Eighth Army.

He struck again on 3 July south of the Ruweisat Ridge, but British 1st Armoured Division, now built up to 119 tanks, were waiting. After one and a half hours, pressed beyond the limits of endurance, the Afrika Corps were brought to a standstill. It cost the British 39 AFVs, but 19th Battalion of 4th New Zealand Brigade overran *Ariete*, Rommel's Italian right flank, capturing 350 POWs and 44 guns.

At nightfall, the three German divisions were down to 1500 men each and the Italians had only five AFVs and two guns. Rommel had had enough for the time being, calling off the offensive to regroup. Reinforcement was necessary before he could resume the attack. At last, Eighth Army had command. In four days Auchinleck transformed a rout into a battle, which Rommel could not win. 3 July was the turning point of the war in North Africa.

BATTLE OF SANTA CRUZ

In 1942 the seemingly unstoppable expansion of Japanese imperialism threatened to engulf the whole of South East Asia and even Australia. Both the Americans and the Japanese had soldiers on the island of Guadalcanal but the Japanese were slow to realize the island's importance, the Imperial Navy being forced to make do with troops already in the south west Pacific. On the American side, Guadalcanal had to compete with the Battle of the Atlantic: it was not surprising that the Marines there thought themselves the forgotten army.

US convoys delivered supplies from Espiritu Santo to the garrison while daylight lasted; at night Japanese troop-carrying destroyers and cruisers would rush down 'the Slot' with reinforcements and stores or to bombard the American positions. Neither side could achieve superiority on the ground, the Japanese were short of supplies, while the Americans found fuel their greatest problem.

The stalemate at Guadalcanal

Then Japan decided to break the stalemate on Guadalcanal, which was also delaying the progress of the New Guinea campaign. The Imperial Staff announced that 'Army and Navy forces will combine and in one action retake Guadalcanal Island airfield.'

During October 1942 the Japanese brought their strength on the island up to 20,000 men. The Americans were fully

The air strikes at Santa Cruz. Naval battles can be very confusing, even more so when aircraft movements are also plotted, giving two dimensions to what is usually a one-dimension chart

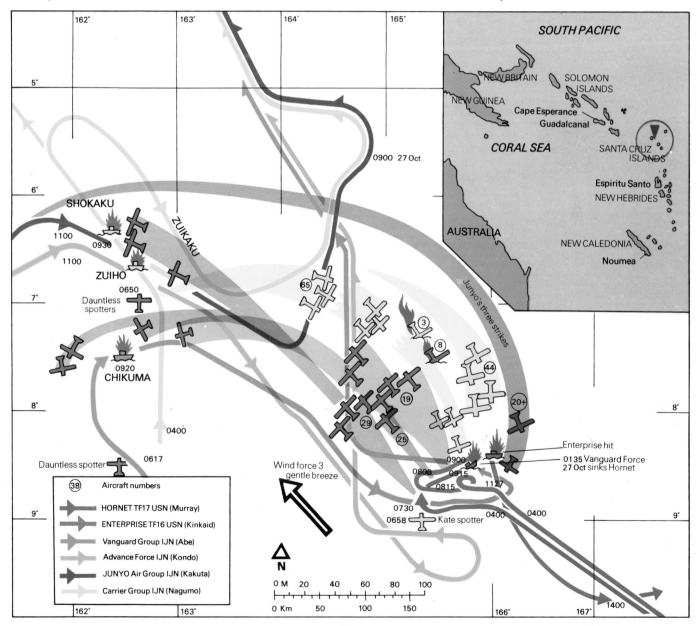

IJN *ZUIKAKU*

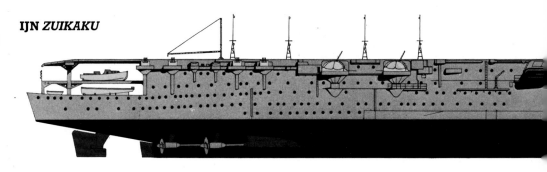

Displacement 25,675 tons
Armour 216 mm (8½ in) main;
171 mm (6¾ in) deck
Armament 36 × 25 mm
(16 × 5 in)
Aircraft 72 operational
Complement 1660
Machinery 8 Kanpon boilers;
turbines gave 160,000 SHP
Speed 34.2 kts
Length 257.5 m (845 ft)
Beam 26 m (85 ft 6 in)
Draught 8.8 m (29 ft)
Laid down Kawasaki, Kobe,
25 May, 1938
Launched 27 November 1939
Sunk 25 October 1944
Sister-ship *Shokaku*;
sunk 19 June 1944

aware of the danger. The US Navy felt that it could not control the sea, supplying US positions could be done only at great military cost. But Washington was prepared to increase its support of South Pacific operations.

The Japanese had planned to capture Henderson Field, the air-base, on 21 October, but the presence of 23,000 Marines and GIs caused postponement until the 23rd. It did them little good, they lost over 2000 men and all their tanks. But the Imperial Navy badly needed fuel and would soon have to withdraw. On 25 October another attack was launched but the Japanese were again forced back. The first part of their plan had failed.

The commander of the South Pacific Area, Admiral William F. Halsey, issued orders to Task Force 64, led by the battleship *Washington*, patrolling west of Savo Island. they said 'Attack-Repeat-Attack' whenever enemy ships were sighted.

Task Force 16 was based on the carrier *Enterprise*, with the battleship *South Dakota*, while another carrier, *Hornet*, led Task Force 17. *South Dakota*, of Task Force 16, was one of a new generation of fast ships, capable of 28 kts, and an armament of nine 16 in guns, Captain Thomas Gatch, her commander, had concentrated on gunnery practice. The battle that followed proved that he had made a trained and efficient

fighting team of his inexperienced ship's company.

The Japanese also divided their combined fleet into a number of units, the two main elements being the Advance Force, led by *Atago* and the Striking Force. The Advance Force was for close support of the troops on Guadalcanal. On 26 October it consisted of two battleships, four heavy cruisers, a destroyer screen, and one carrier, *Junyo*. The Striking Force, to deal with the US Fleet, was sub-divided into a group of three aircraft-carriers and their screen and a force of three heavy cruisers and destroyers. The carriers *Shokaku* and *Zuikaku* were to work with the *Yamato*-class super-battleships.

Within the main divisions of the fleet the carriers operated as a unit, without support except destroyers. This made it easier to co-ordinate aircraft operations, but it left the carriers exposed to air attack.

Just another fine day . . .
Dawn on 26 October revealed a fine day, with enough cloud to conceal a dive-bomber attack. The American carriers were north of the Santa Cruz islands. Their course was north-west and less than 320 km (200 miles) ahead were the Japanese forces in a triangular formation, the Vanguard Group of the Striking Force leading the carriers by 95 km (60 miles). One hundred

SS *HORNET*

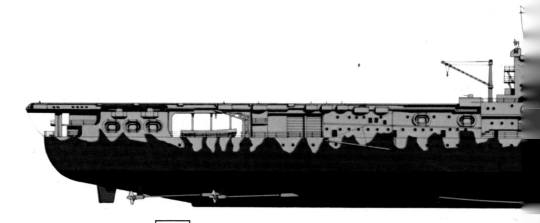

Displacement 20,000 tons
Armour 102 mm (4 in) main;
77 mm (3 in) deck
Armament 8 × 5 in AA
16 × 1.1 in AA
16 × 5 in MGs
Aircraft Approx 100
Complement 2200
Machinery turbines, four-shaft
geared, giving 120,000 SHP
Speed 34 kts
Length 245 m (809½ ft)
Beam 30 m (100 ft)
Draught 7.9 m (26 ft)
Laid down Newport News,
Virginia, 1938
Launched 14 December 1940
Sunk 27 October 1942
Sister-ships *Yorktown*
Launched 4 April 1936;
sunk 7 June 1942
Enterprise
Launched 3 October 1936;
scrapped Kearny, September
1958
Hornet's aircraft were
engaged in the Tokyo raid,
18 April 1942

GRUMMAN 'WILDCAT' F4F-4

Engine One Pratt and Whitney
R1830 radial giving 1200 hp
Armament Six .5 in Browning
MGs; 2 100 lb bombs
Span 11.5 m (38 ft)
Length 8.5 m (28 ft 9 in)
Height 2.8 m (9 ft 2½ in)
Range 1239 km (770 miles)
Speed 512 k/h (318 mph)

There is no denying the bravery of the Japanese pilots in the Pacific war. Here a 'Kate' torpedo-bomber ignores an American cruiser as it hurtles towards the vessel carrying the war photographer

UNITED STATES SOUTH PACIFIC FORCE		JAPANESE COMBINED FLEET	
Comsopac	**Vice-Adm. Halsey**	**C-in-C (at Truk)**	**Adm. Yamamoto in Yamato**
TASK FORCE 16	Rear-Adm. Kinkaid	**ADVANCE FORCE**	Vice-Adm. Kondo
Aircraft Carrier (1)	**Enterprise**; Air Group 10	Cruisers (5)	Atago Takao Myoko Mayo
83 aircraft	34 F4F-4 Grumman Wildcats		Isuzu
	36 SBD-3 Douglas Dauntless	Destroyers (6)	Naganami Makinami Takanami
	dive bombers		Umikaze Kawakaze Suzukaze
	13 TBF-1 Grumman Avenger	**Air Group**	Rear-Adm. Kakuta
	torpedo bombers	Aircraft Carrier (1)	**Junyo**
Battleship (1)	South Dakota	55 aircraft	24 Mitsubishi A6M ('Zeke')
Cruisers (2)	Portland San Juan (AA)		Zero fighters
Destroyers (8)	Porter Mahan Cushing		21 Aichi D3A ('Val')
	Preston Smith Maury		dive bombers
	Conyngham Shaw		10 Nakajima B5N ('Kate')
			torpedo bombers
TASK FORCE 17	Rear-Adm. Murray	Destroyers (2)	Kuroshio Hayashio
Aircraft Carrier (1)	**Hornet**; Air Group 8	**Support Group**	Vice-Adm. Kurita
88 aircraft	36 F4F-4 36-SBD-3	Battleships (2)	Kongo Haruna
	16 TBF-1	Destroyers (6)	Samidare Yudachi Harusame
Cruisers (4)	Northampton Pensacola		Oyashio Kagero Murasame
	San Diego Juneau (AA)		
Destroyers (6)	Morris Anderson Hughes	**STRIKING FORCE**	Vice-Adm. Nagumo
	Mustin Russell Barton	**Carrier Group**	
		Aircraft Carriers (3)	**Shokaku** 18 'Zeke' 20 'Val'
Total ships = 23 warships	**Total aircraft** = 171	61 aircraft	23 'Kate'
		72 aircraft	**Zuikaku** 27 'Zeke' 27 'Val'
			18 'Kate'
		24 aircraft	**Zuiho** 18 'Zeke' 6 'Kate'
		Cruisers (1)	Kumano
		Destroyers (8)	Amatsukaze Hatsukaze
			Tokitsukaze Yukikaze
			Arashi Maikaze Teruzuki
			Hamamaze
		Vanguard Group	Rear-Adm. Abe
		Battleships (2)	Hiei Kirishima
		Cruisers (4)	Nagara Tone Chikuma
			Suzuya
		Destroyers (7)	Kazagumo Makigumo Yugumo
			Akigumo Tanikaze Urakaze
			Isokaze
		Total ships = 47 warships	
		Total aircraft = 212	

and sixty kilometres (100 miles) west was the Advanced Force, with the carrier *Junyo* even farther west. The whole force was steering north. And both sides were well aware of the enemy's presence.

Rear Admiral Thomas Kinkaid ordered an air search from *Enterprise*. Sixteen Dauntless dive-bombers took off, fanning out in pairs to the north and west, and at 0617 the Vanguard Group was sighted. Then at 0740 two Dauntlesses attacked the light carrier *Zuiho* and hit it.

Japanese aircraft had identified a US task force at 0658. At 0700 a 65-strong group of Kates, Kekes and Vals took off. At 0730 15 Dauntless, six Avenger torpedo bombers and eight Wildcat fighters left *Hornet*. *Enterprise*'s first strike consisted of eight Avengers, eight wildcats and three Dauntlesses, flying off at 0800, followed at 1815 by *Hornet*'s second strike of 26 aircraft.

The US aircraft passed the incoming Japanese strike. Some Japanese fighters left their group to attack the Americans; four Wildcats and four Avengers were either shot down or severely damaged and forced back to *Enterprise*, halving the US strike.

The US Fleet was ready for the attack. Aircraft were secured below, fuel lines were filled with carbon dioxide, damage control parties were on constant alert. Speed was held at 28 kts and the escort screen were poised to give massive AA fire. First line of defence was 38 Wildcats, directed from *Enterprise*. But for some time the fighter-direction team could not distinguish between American and Japanese

Top left One Kamikazi that missed! Aircraft and bomb explode in the sea as an American cruiser takes avoiding action

Below left The air is filled with AA bursts of shredded steel as the doomed USS *Hornet* comes under determined attack

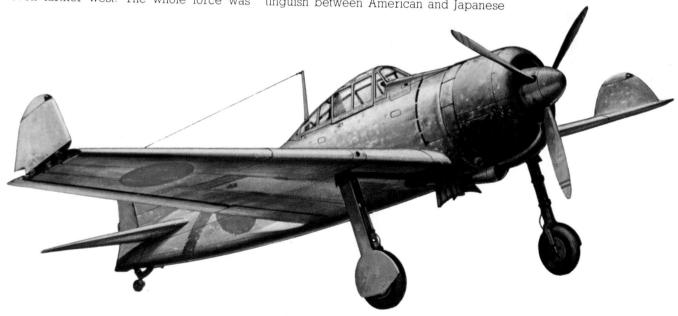

MITSUBISHI A6M2 AERO	**Armament** Two 20 mm cannon; 2 7.7 mm MGs	**Height** 3 m (10 ft)
Engine One Nakajima NK1C Sakae 12, 14-cylinder radial	**Span** 12 m (39 ft 4½ in) **Length** 9 m (29 ft 8¾ in)	**Range** 3106 km (1930 miles) with drop-tank **Speed** 534 k/h (332 mph)

The signal bridge of the *Hornet*, left a pile of scorched and twisted steel after a suicide dive by a crippled Japanese plane. But it was not long before the true Kamikaze suicide squads took to the air to throw their lives away in cold and deliberate self-destruction, flying in aircraft that carried only enough fuel to get them to their targets

aircraft. It was 0857 before a clear picture emerged. At first neither the Wildcats nor the AA fire could break the co-ordination of the Japanese attack.

Suicide run by a burning Kate

At about 0900 *Enterprise*'s group was hidden by a rain squall. This left *Hornet* to face the full weight of the Japanese attack. Val dive-bombers began the assault, scoring a hit and two near-misses. Their squadron commander aimed his Val right at the carrier's funnel, it hit and burnt through the flight deck. This attack covered the approach of Kate torpedo bombers from astern. Two torpedoes hit *Hornet*'s engine room and she slowed to a halt. Three more bombs hit, then a burning Kate made another suicide run into the port side. It was all over in ten minutes. The Japanese lost 25 planes, but the formidable *Hornet* was a listing, blazing wreck.

Now, the American aircraft were nearing the Japanese fleet. Disturbed by fighters, they were unable to deliver a united attack, or even find the same target. Fifteen Dauntlesses led the attack. The first wave of Japanese defending fighters was kept at bay by the Wildcats. But 11 bombers got through and hit *Shokaku* about five times, the 450 kg (1000 lb) bombs tearing her flight-deck open and starting a tremendous fire in the hangar. *Zuiho* went unmolested. At 0930 the Avengers unsuccessfully attacked the cruiser *Suzuya*.

Hornet's second wave damaged the cruiser *Chikuma* but *Enterprise*'s aircraft had no luck at all. As the US aircraft turned for home the result of the battle was in the balance. Two Japanese carriers were out of action, but the second strike from *Shokaku* and *Zuikaku* had not yet attacked. *Junyo* was hurrying west and *Shokaku* was out of action.

On the US side, *Hornet*'s fires had been brought under control, although the order to abandon ship had been given. By 1005 the cruiser *Northampton* was starting to tow the carrier. Although Task Force 16 had not yet been attacked, it was a scene of increasing confusion. Above were stacked the surviving aircraft from both carriers, now nearing the end of their fuel.

Then the second Japanese strike was detected. *Enterprise* prepared to defend herself, but the attack was not well co-ordinated, the dive-bombers arriving 20 minutes after the torpedo-bombers, and they were met by the heaviest AA barrage yet seen in the Pacific. *South Dakota* shot down 26 Vals, *Enterprise* claimed another seven. But two bombs found their mark, damaging the flight deck and starting more fires in the hangar.

Enterprise's brilliant avoiding action

When the torpedo-bombers arrived they were attacked by the US fighters, but about 14 got through. Five were destroyed by AA fire, but the rest closed in on *Enterprise* from both sides, the carrier taking brilliant avoiding action. The crew struggled to clear the flight deck and recover circling aircraft before they ran out of fuel. Then at 1101 *Junyo*'s strike appeared on radar, but hidden in cloud. Twenty attacked, achieving one near miss but losing eight planes. Two Vals dived on *South Dakota* and

the AA ship *San Juan*. A bomb exploded on the battleship's foremost turret but did not penetrate.

The tight formation of Task Force 16 was shattered, but the carrier was able to recover aircraft even though her forward elevator was out of action. The Japanese had two carriers left but had lost over 100 aircraft. Their battleship squadrons increased speed, hoping to finish off the crippled US ships. *Northampton*, still inching *Hornet* to safety, was spotted at 1515 by Japanese aircraft, so she cut the tow, leaving the carrier an easy target. One torpedo was enough, and the survivors were taken off. Destroyers fired nine torpedoes into her and over 400 5 in shells. But she was still afloat, burning from end to end, when the Japanese found her, and they had the satisfaction of giving the *coup de grace*.

Neither side suffered decisive losses, the US lost *Hornet* and a destroyer, with four ships damaged. No major Japanese vessel had been sunk, but two carriers and a destroyer were out of action. American aircraft losses were 20 destroyed and 54 missing or damaged; the Japanese lost 100.

By the time the Japanese carrier fleet had been repaired and re-equipped it was too late to save Guadalcanal. Santa Cruz might have been a setback for the US, but it bought time to ensure final victory in the Pacific.

Top ship in this interesting photograph is the 35,000-ton battleship USS *South Dakota*, which had been hit on the corner of the forward triple 16 in gun-turret during the battle of Santa Cruz. Splinters from the bomb wounded the ship's commander, Capt. Gatch, as he stood on the bridge. No. 2 turret is depressed as the guns are overhauled before the Guadalcanal battle to come. The 207 m (680 ft) long battleship is lying alongside USS *Prometheus*, special repair-ship at anchor off Noumea

THE ORAN LANDINGS

The outcome of World War 2 was in the balance in mid-1942. The Axis powers were fighting the British in the Middle East without fearing for the security of their Libyan base. They could not be attacked from the west and north-west because French Morocco, Algeria and Tunisia were under control of the pro-nazi Vichy government.

Winston Churchill agreed to President Roosevelt's suggestion on 25 July for a landing in Morocco, but there were arguments between British and American commanders about the best places for a landing. US demands prevailed for Casablanca and General Dwight D. Eisenhower was given command of Operation Torch.

The military forces would be mostly American, Vichy France would be less hostile to them than the British, but the naval strength would be British.

Torch committed Americans directly to the fight against Germany and Italy and not only against Japan. Torch convinced Hitler and Mussolini that Britain and her Empire no longer stood alone. Militarily it could hardly be more important. This was the Americans' first land engagement of the war in the European theatre and much depended on their showing.

How would the French react?

D-day was fixed for 8 November. Would the 150,000 Vichy French, Zouaves, Algerians and French Foreign Legion resist the landings? With many casualties the French would turn against the Allies. The destruction of French battleships at Oran by the Royal Navy on 3-4 July 1940 had already enbittered many Frenchmen. Secret talks with some French officers sympathetic to the Allies were held. It saved many British and American lives and brought many Vichy French over to the Allies.

By 6 November, the invasion forces were at sea in three great convoys totally 650 ships, only one being lost by enemy action

before the landing. Royal Navy Intelligence had done their job of security and deception so skilfully that enemy observers saw nothing to suggest any imminent major operation.

Leading was Eastern Task Force, with 33,000 men, including British, in 34 transports escorted by 25 Royal Navy warships. Its job was to capture Algiers, seaport capital of Algeria. Behind was Centre Task Force, with 39,000 Americans in 47 transports, heading for Oran, Algeria's second city. Escort was 25 Royal Navy vessels.

From the US came Western Task Force, 35,000 men in 39 transports protected by 47 US warships. The main attack would be at Fedala, near Morocco's largest city Casablanca, with flanking attacks at Port Lyautey, north, and Safi in the south.

The assault on the Oran sector was the key. By the afternoon of 7 November, Centre Task Force had grouped into operational columns, dividing after nightfall and turning south to close on their landing beaches.

Fifty kilometres (30 miles) west was 'X' beach, near the Mersa Bou Zedjarr headland—the target of the armoured task force of 2250 men of Colonel Paul Robinett. Brigadier General Theodore Roosevelt (son of the 1901 President) would land 5000 of his 26th Regimental combat team at 'Y' beach 19 km (12 miles) west of Oran. The same distance east was 'Z' beach, objective of the main strike force: 15,400 men under General Lloyd Fredenhall. From 'X' and 'Y' on one

US troops cross the beach at Oran near Arzew. Just behind the colour bearer with the Stars and Stripes is a mortar team. The US flag was displayed in the hope that the Vichy French would be less likely to fight. The area was secured by the 3rd Battalion, 18th Regimental Combat Team, which joined two other battalions

A US 40 mm light AA gun is towed ashore on to 'Z' beach, east of Oran. To the right is an RN mechanized landing craft (LCM64). These 21-ton craft could carry a vehicle of under 16 tons or two 37 mm AT guns and carriers, or six jeeps or 100 troops. They could be hoisted on and off-ship by derrick

side and 'Z' on the other the plan was an overlapping pincer movement to crush Oran.

Dead in the middle of Centre Task Force, making for Oran's harbour, were HMS *Walney* and *Hartland*, each carrying about 200 men of the US 6th Armored Infantry with orders to capture the harbour, naval vessels, batteries and barracks, to stop Vichy French demolition and scuttling of ships.

Now the three-pronged attack closed on the dark Algerian coast. Vichy French HQ observed the convoys but decided that they were heading for the eastern Mediterranean.

Americans had no landing techniques

As yet, the Americans had evolved no landing techniques, so the standard British procedure was used. A beacon submarine was sent ahead to mark the rendezvous for transports. As each one came up it sent a launch to the sub to collect the pilot, who took the big ship closer in. Then the sub moved inshore and sent teams in small boats to take station close to the beach and show 'aiming lights' for the landing craft to home in on. There were natural obstacles, rocks and soft, sliding sand, but the system worked well.

By 0131, 'Y' beach landing craft were reaching the shore. An assault company

moved to the dunes on the landward side and established a forward line. Next, assault engineers marked assembly areas for units and vehicles, and dumps for supplies.

Brigadier General Roosevelt's five combat team transports contacted their beacon on schedule and had their first landing craft in the water about midnight.

At 'X' beach the landing was unopposed and by 0900 an armoured battalion, a tank destroyer platoon and an engineer battalion were on the road to Oran. Though the landing was trouble-free, the first three landing craft ran on to a sandbar and jeeps and guns disappeared into deep water on the landward side. However, half the troops and 33 vehicles were soon ashore. An AT platoon was in position at El Ancor a mile inland. Fredenhall learned that he would soon have troops in the hills above the Plain of Andalous. First enemy contact came at 0800 when American AT gunners knocked out three French armoured cars at point-blank range.

In the 'Z' beach area their landings went with clinical precision. While men and equipment got ashore from 34 transports, men of the 1st Ranger Battalion went straight to the small port of Arzew, caught the garrison asleep and captured the coastal battery. A mile away, Rangers climbed

BRITISH LANDING SHIP TANK (CONVERTED LAKE MARACAIBO TANKER)

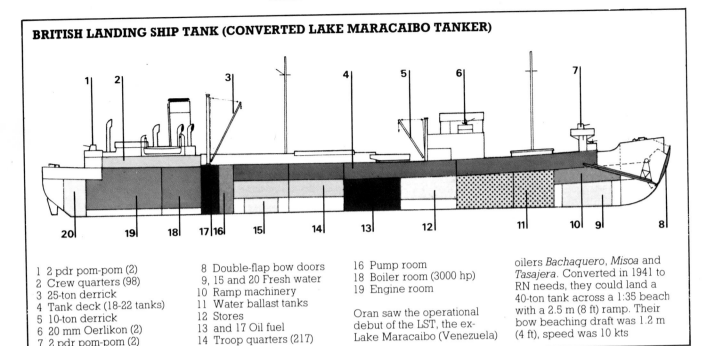

1 2 pdr pom-pom (2)
2 Crew quarters (98)
3 25-ton derrick
4 Tank deck (18-22 tanks)
5 10-ton derrick
6 20 mm Oerlikon (2)
7 2 pdr pom-pom (2)

8 Double-flap bow doors
9, 15 and 20 Fresh water
10 Ramp machinery
11 Water ballast tanks
12 Stores
13 and 17 Oil fuel
14 Troop quarters (217)

16 Pump room
18 Boiler room (3000 hp)
19 Engine room

Oran saw the operational debut of the LST, the ex-Lake Maracaibo (Venezuela)

oilers *Bachaquero*, *Misoa* and *Tasajera*. Converted in 1941 to RN needs, they could land a 40-ton tank across a 1:35 beach with a 2.5 m (8 ft) ramp. Their bow beaching draft was 1.2 m (4 ft), speed was 10 kts

cliffs to attack a powerful, fortified 105 mm battery. Marines followed the Rangers into Arzew to take the barracks and naval base, including 13 seaplanes fuelled up and armed with torpedoes.

Allied naval assault hits trouble

The operation was going fine, but the naval assault in the centre had run into terrible trouble. This part of Torch called for a frontal assault on the strongly defended port. Complete surprise was essential—yet the attack was made at 0245, *after* the beach landings, a major error for the Oran defences were fully alert. Their disciplined troops held fire. Captain F. T. Peters, commanding Centre Task Force, took *Walney* and *Hartland* in, both ships wearing the White Ensign and large American flags.

Suddenly searchlights flared and heavy automatic fire struck the ships. Peters pressed on under cover of smoke, broke the boom and entered harbour, but a French sloop *La Surprise* fired her guns at point-blank range with devastating effect. Her engines wrecked and her decks littered with dead and dying men, *Walney* drifted up-harbour. Crossfire from French submarines and AA destroyer hit her, a few survivors abandoned ship, then she capsized and sank. *Hartland*, too, was hit and sank.

The naval operation suffered appalling casualties. Peters was posthumously awarded the VC, and the American DSC went to Commander Godfrey Billot of *Hartland*. Later, British naval actions were successful. *Le Surprise* left port to engage the Allied transports and was sunk by the cruiser *Aurora* and another French ship was forced back into port.

War's most incompetent airborne assault

The airborne assault on Oran must rank as one of the most incompetent airborne operations of the war. The paratroops of 2nd Battalion, US 503rd Regiment, were told the night before that unopposed landings were expected. Take-off was postponed until 2200, rain and fog hindered the pilots. Radio contact was poor over the Spanish mountains and they lost formation. A ship sending a homing signal used the wrong frequency, and a signal that landings would be opposed was never received.

Scattered and low on fuel, the planes approached the North African coast just before daybreak. Six flew too far west, one landed at Gibraltar, two in French Morocco and three in Spanish Morocco. But 32 arrived over Algeria, then 12 dropped their men 30 km (20 miles) off target. Most of the transport planes landed at the wrong end of Salt Lake. Some empty planes, together with one with its load of paratroops landed on salt flats south of Oran. All the Americans on board were taken prisoner without a fight—by French civilian police. The GIs were not sure if they could shoot at the French!

The Allied air assault was more successful. About 70 French aircraft were destroyed on the ground, and French air action was limited to attempts to defend airfields. No serious attacks were made on the landings.

Some opposition stiffened, coastal batteries shelled the transports and forced them farther out, armour began to blunt the American probes. The only serious opposition was at Misserhin and Valmy, both of which were by-passed. By late on 9 November strong American groups were in position for a concentric attack on Oran, to start at 0715 on 10 November.

At first the assault was slowed by shellfire, but US artillery and British naval guns silenced the French. At French HQ General Emile Boissau was induced—at the point of a handgun—to accept terms for an armistice.

At Algiers the Allies faced the least trouble. Vichy troops repelled one attempted landing from the harbour, but aided by Free French, the British 11th Infantry Brigade of Eastern Task Force quickly overcame resistance. Admiral Jean Darland, Commander-in-Chief of the Vichy armed forces was taken into protective custody.

Along the Moroccan coast, Safi was taken quickly, but fighting around Casablanca and Port Lyautey was fierce. At both places the invading troops were greatly helped by accurate naval fire. In Casablanca the unfinished battleship *Jean Bart* used her four 15 in guns to duel with the US battleship *Massachusetts*. The French destroyer flotilla, supported by a cruiser, met the full strength of the US Fleet and seven ships and three submarines were sunk, with 1000 casualties.

On 9 November the beachheads were secure. Next day the Americans advanced on Casablanca and after heavy fighting all day the defenders capitulated.

Hitler reacted promptly by ordering the occupation of Vichy France. It caused the scuttling of the French fleet at Toulon. The Axis concentrated U-boat attacks on the traffic which began to flow to the Allied bases in Morocco and Algeria, but it was too late.

Torch launched the GI into land battle: it was the beginning of the end for the Germans and Italians in North Africa. The Allies could now concentrate on Europe.

Left F4F Wildcat fighters of the carrier USS *Ranger* test their six .5 in Browning MGs during Western Task Force's voyage to Morocco. The Wildcats' unit markings have been erased by the wartime censor

Below The heavy cruiser USS *Augusta* fires its triple 8 in guns at Fedala, near Morocco's largest city Casablanca. The town would be the centre of General Patton's main attack

This chapter, for the year 1943, contains but two battles. Of course, in such a widespread war there are a number of battles, of which many could find a place here. Such a battle was fought at Stalingrad, when no fewer than 40,000 Germans surrendered after losing 110,500 dead; or the action at the Kasserine Pass, where General Rommel's genius produced a severe blow to untested American troops.

The air war too was beginning to hit Germany. Daylight raids on Berlin by six RAF Mosquitoes interrupted broadcast speeches by Goering and Goebbels. The bombs fell as the two German leaders spoke about the tenth anniversary of the Nazi regime.

Two years into this war the dreadful Russian bloodbath of Barbarossa had continued unabated since the Wehrmacht had invaded Germany's erstwhile ally. In July, a gigantic tank battle took place at Kursk. Hitler's codeword for the action was Operation Zitadelle, signifying that his Ninth Army and Fourth Panzer Army must not fail him there, the 'citadel' must stand firm. Hitler's message to his soldiers was: 'The future of the war may depend on this battle's outcome.' And he was right, but his army was not up to the task. The Battle of Kursk became known as the 'Death Ride of the Panzers', in which 20 Panzer divisions were decimated. Ultimately it heralded the failure of Germany to overrun Russia. This titanic struggle exposed war for its ability to bring man to his knees in awful desolation and dreadful exhaustion. This was Kursk. The Germans lost their strength and with it the ability to continue fighting against an adversary who retained his drive and was backed by seemingly limitless resources and manpower.

The frightful carnage at Stalingrad was coming to an end with the surrender of 40,000 more Germans. This struggle for the city had cost Germany 110,500 dead; the Russian defenders, military and civilian, had to bury a million.

In the Mediterranean, the war was just beginning to go the Allies' way. In July the Allies launched Operation Husky to drive the Germans from Sicily, the toe of Italy and the gateway to Europe. As a seaborne assault it was bigger even than the eventual Normandy invasion to come in 1944. The Seventh US Army was ranged alongside the Eighth British Army, both under the Supreme Commander, General Dwight D. Eisenhower.

Sicily duly fell, but the successful landing was not followed up. Why some 40,000 German troops were allowed to get away is one of the more embarrassing stories from World War 2 in the Mediterranean. One plus-point did, however, come from Operation Husky: it led to Benito Mussolini's eventual downfall and assassination, the end of Italy as an Axis partner, and made the area safe for Allied shipping.

This year also saw the completion of the 'Death Railway' in Burma. Driven cruelly by their Japanese captors, it was built by British, Australian, US and Dutch POWs and when the last sleeper was laid in place the line was littered with 93,000 dead, including 12,000 Allied soldiers.

The second battle in this chapter describes the end of another kind of titan. It was the German Navy's vaunted 32,000-ton battleship *Scharnhorst*. Well armed and fast, she could, single-handed, destroy any Allied convoy and its escorts and her presence in the Atlantic was a threat not to be ignored. In an attempt to strike at a Murmansk-bound convoy she fell foul of forces her equal and was destroyed with all but 36 of her 2000-man crew.

As this year ended, General Eisenhower was appointed Supreme Commander for the invasion of Europe, with Air Chief Marshal Tedder, RAF, as his Deputy. The Allies knew now that the war would go their way.

In March, Field Marshal Eric von Manstein's great victory at Kharkov for Army Group South suggested that their Russian campaign might be going Germany's way. But it was short-lived. A great Russian bulge penetrated some 120 km (75 miles) westward into the German lines at Kursk, with a base measuring more than 160 km (100 miles) from north to south. Within the salient were a million men and their armour. A German pincer movement across the base would cut off and destroy the forces in it and weaken the Soviet Army. Manstein planned such a move to clinch his victory.

Then the weather took a hand. The spring came and vast tracts of frozen ground turned to mud. Manstein had to withdraw his armour to save it from getting bogged down. But the longer the Germans remained on the defensive the sooner would the Russians take the initiative to widen the salient and breach the German front.

Speed and decisiveness would have produced results, but the German High Command hesitated. By 11 April they realized that their only chance lay in an unstoppable assault. It meant risking far more armour than the Germans could

Far left The Eastern Front in July 1943

Left Field Marshal Eric von Manstein, commander of Army Group South. At Kursk, Manstein was forced to conduct a set-piece battle not of his choosing

Inset Lt. General Josef (Sepp) Dietrich. An Oberst-gruppenfuehrer of the SS *Liebstandarte Adolf Hitler* Division at Kursk, Dietrich was a crony of Hitler and backed his judgement to go ahead with the Kursk attack against strong opposition. His unit destroyed 27 T34 Red Army tanks at Gremutshy. In 1944-5 he commanded the 6th Panzer Army

Below The ravages of war show clearly on this German soldier's face. His campaign ribbons show he has seen plenty of service. But now he is exhausted and battle-weary

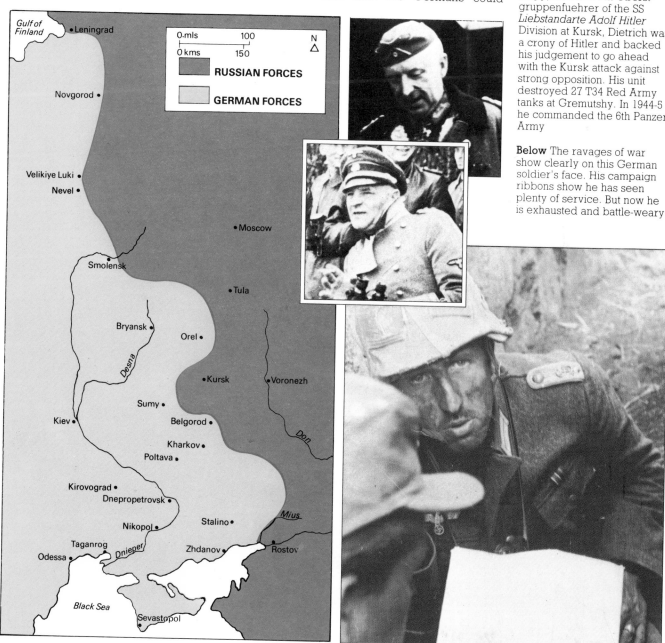

RUSSIAN FORCES

GERMAN FORCES

afford, and if infantry support was needed it also meant weakening the front north and south. Hitler hesitated again. But the Russians did not, going ahead with the preparation for a large-scale counter-attack. Then on 10 May Hitler at last gave his consent to Operation *Zitadelle*.

Pincer arms are poised

The forces were decided. Walther Model's Ninth Army, with seven Panzer, two Panzer-genadier and nine infantry divisions would attack from the north; Heinz Hoth's Fourth Panzer Army, with ten Panzer, a Panzer-grenadier and seven infantry divisions would sweep up from the south. The two arms of the pincer would meet east of Kursk, cutting off huge Russian forces.

Then Hitler again postponed the start, from 13 June to the beginning of July, so that Panther AFVs could be sent to boost Model's northern pincer. The opening of the greatest tank battle in history was finally fixed for 1500 on 4 July.

Opposing the Germans were 11 Russian Armies, including the crack Sixth and Seventh Guards Armies and First Tank Army. Each Russian 'army' matched a German corps. Both conflicting forces were nearly equal in manpower. The Russians had reinforced the north corner of the salient which would bear the brunt of Model's attack with thickly sown mines, 20,000 guns, 6000 AT guns and over 900 *Katyusha* rocket launchers. The Germans relied on the new Panther D AFV and they

had air superiority, with squadrons of Stukas.

The battle would be fought over ideal tank-warfare ground. Kursk lies in the basins of the Don and Dneiper. There are many brooks and rivers, cornfields stretch across the landscape and roads are cart tracks.

Hoth's army extended 50 km (30 miles) west to east: 3rd and 11th Panzer Divisions, the *Gross Deutschland* Division, three SS divisions, *Leibstandarte Adolf Hitler*, *Totenkopf* and *Das Reich*. On the right wing were 6th, 19th, and 7th Panzer divisions. Tanks were moved into position at night. German morale was high. A message from Hitler was read: 'Soldiers of the Reich! This day you are to take part in an offensive of such importance that the whole future of the war may depend upon it. . . . Your victory will show the whole world that resistance to the power of the German army is hopeless.'

But the message came during a four hour bombardment, not, however, affecting the 1500 start as planned. By 1900 the German left flank had thrust into the Russian forward lines, but the Red Army was luring them into an untenable position.

Panzers v Russian mines

Model's northern pincer broke 25 km (15 miles) into the salient, but at great cost in assault tanks. During the next week, the Model thrust could only gain a further 8 km (5 miles), the thick Russian mine-fields causing many casualties.

The Flammerwerfer PzKfw III, a flame-thrower version of the Panzer III. It carried 1000 l (250 gal) of flame fuel. The AFV weighed 23 tons and had a range of over 36.5 km (60 miles). While only 100 Panzer IIIs were converted in this way, a number fought at Kursk with the 11th Panzer Division

FLAMMENWERFER PZKFW 111

In the south, Hoth's forces gained ground, but only at serious cost. An overnight cloudburst turned the ground into a morass, stopping tanks moving into line. Stuka attacks had some success against the Red artillery, but early on 5 July the AFVs faced serious trouble. The whole of 48 Panzer Corps got bogged down on open ground and became targets for air attack.

On higher ground, the three SS divisions had more luck, knocking out 27 T34s and avoiding trouble. The Russians thought the

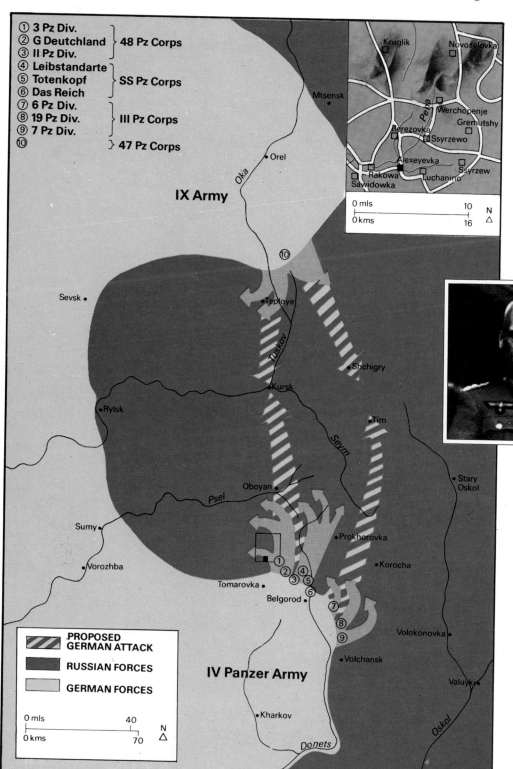

① 3 Pz Div.
② G Deutchland } 48 Pz Corps
③ II Pz Div.
④ Leibstandarte
⑤ Totenkopf } SS Pz Corps
⑥ Das Reich
⑦ 6 Pz Div.
⑧ 19 Pz Div. } III Pz Corps
⑨ 7 Pz Div.
⑩ } 47 Pz Corps

IX Army

IV Panzer Army

PROPOSED GERMAN ATTACK
RUSSIAN FORCES
GERMAN FORCES

0 mls 40
0 kms 70
N

0 mls 10
0 kms 16
N

Below Col. General Paul Hausser, commander of the 2nd SS Panzer Corps, elite of the best-equipped Panzer divisions. In 1944 he commanded the Seventh Army in Normandy

Left The Kursk salient, showing the proposed German pincer movement through the Russian forces in July 1943 and their actual progress. German units are numbered

Inset Col. General Heinz Hoth, the commander of the Fourth Panzer Army. He was the longest serving Panzer general and commanded the southern pincer movement during the Kursk offensive. Hoth was dismissed after the fall of Kiev in November 1943

Right General N. F. Vatutin, who was described by Marshal Zhukov as a brilliant and courageous soldier. His political aide in 1943 was Nikita Khruschev. Vatutin died in mysterious circumstances at Kiev in 1944

Below The SU152 heavy assault gun, nicknamed 'Conquering Beast' by the Red Army. Weighing 50 tons, its 152 mm howitzer had a 14.5 km (9 mile) range. This SPG made its battle debut in the Kursk fighting

Germans had suffered heavy losses and so were not prepared for a German attack, which was eventually halted. The day ended with stalemate.

On the third day the sun had dried the swampy ground and the Germans had some success on their southern pincer. But the minefields had created terrible losses, with bodies strewn over the battlefield. Then 48 Panzer Corps attacked in the north-west, broke through and caused havoc among the Seventh Guards Army, which fled in disorder.

Gross Deutschland wheeled round to Ssyrzewo, catching the Russians by surprise. Then a counter-attack by the Red Army brought 500 tanks face to face, firing point-blank at each other until the battlefield was littered with blazing AFVs. No ground

had been gained by either side. It was just a terrible waste of men and machines.

After a week, the German pincer forces were near exhausted, short of ammunition and supplies. Again and again the invading army tried to make headway. But not even the Luftwaffe could deal with the huge numbers of Russian AFVs. Their losses were replaced with magical rapidity, supplies were endless. But there was no sign of supplies for the Germans, whose AFVs had been cut by more than half.

German armour reaches the end

Hitler had put in hazard more armour than he could afford to lose. The battle's climax came during 12-14 July. For nine days Germans and Russians had been slugging at each other, neither achieving a knock-out. Hoth called for a last attempt, but he had only 600 AFVs as a spearhead, and every soldier was exhausted. In contrast, the Russians had fresh men and plenty of new tanks. The last attack came on 12 July. 'Let us finish the issue of Kursk once and for all!' said Hoth. His words led to the 'Death Ride of the Panzer Army', as the action became known.

Burning wrecks soon covered the battle-field, as from the hills the Russian artillery pounded the German forces. Suddenly the order came from Hitler: 'Operation *Zitadelle* is cancelled.' It presaged the end of the German invasion of Russia. The Kursk gambit was a German move that failed.

SU152 'CONQUERING BEAST'

LAVOCHKIN LA5FN

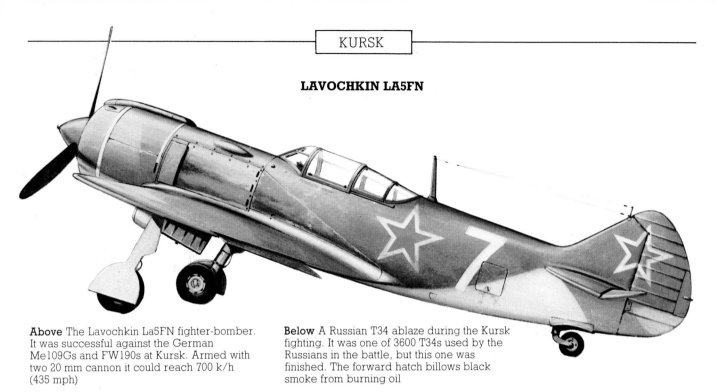

Above The Lavochkin La5FN fighter-bomber. It was successful against the German Me109Gs and FW190s at Kursk. Armed with two 20 mm cannon it could reach 700 k/h (435 mph)

Below A Russian T34 ablaze during the Kursk fighting. It was one of 3600 T34s used by the Russians in the battle, but this one was finished. The forward hatch billows black smoke from burning oil

DEATH OF THE *SCHARNHORST*

Scharnhorst was probably the Royal Navy's most hated enemy. She had sunk the armed merchant cruiser *Rawalpindi*, the aircraft carrier *Glorious* and the destroyers *Ardent* and *Acasta* with dreadful loss of life. Even while holed up in Northern Norway she was a threat, forcing powerful Royal Navy units to cover Murmansk convoys. In the Atlantic, *Scharnhorst* could do more damage to a convoy than a whole pack of U-boats.

Rear Admiral Erich Bey came from the

Tirpitz, which had been crippled by a British midget-submarine attack on 24 December. At 1400 he ordered, 'Make ready for sea.' A British convoy had been reported, Murmansk-bound with arms for Russia. In severe weather, Bey took *Scharnhorst* out with a five-destroyer escort. Target was Convoy JW55B. As they left port in a blizzard and mountainous seas, HQ signalled Bey: 'Attack and destroy the convoy to alleviate the struggle of your

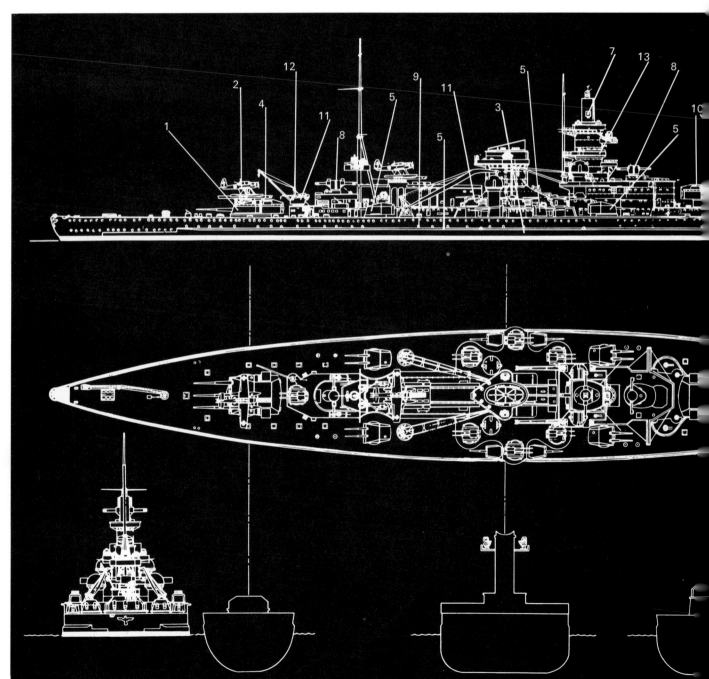

comrades on the Eastern Front.'

The 19 ships of Convoy JW55B had a close escort of two corvettes and 15 destroyers, led by Captain J. A. McCoy in *Onslow*, supported by three cruisers under Vice-Admiral R. Burnett in *Belfast*, with *Sheffield* and *Norfolk* in company.

The Germans thought that this was all the convoy's protection—*Scharnhorst* could deal with them all, and the British destroyers would be ineffectual in the heavy seas. The Germans knew the exact position of the convoy at 0900 on 25 December, as U-boats informed on the ships' movements. Bey planned to hit the convoy at first light, but the Arctic winter is an uncertain time, daylight is near non-existent.

But the Germans did not know that on 24 December Admiral Sir Bruce Fraser, Commander-in-Chief Home Fleet, had ordered the convoy on a reverse course for three hours and increased its speed. These factors were to seriously affect the German calculations.

A bad-weather report from *U601* led HQ to call off the attack. Then Doenitz ordered it to go on. Among the German signals a vital

Below The battleship *Scharnhorst* after her launching in 1937. The straight bows were given a clipper rake just before war broke out in 1939

Bottom The Royal Navy's battleship *Duke of York* on her return to port after the successful battle against the *Scharnhorst* on 26 December 1943. The crew are mustered on deck waiting to go ashore

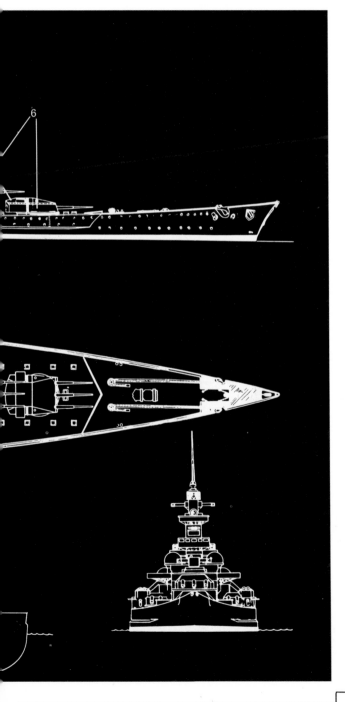

SCHARNHORST

1 Rear turret, 11 in
2 Arado spotter plane
3 Belt armour: 305 mm (12 in)
4 Plane catapult
5 Secondary 5.9 in guns
6 Front turrets, 11 in
7 Main range-finder
8 Second range-finder
9 Deck armour, 152 mm (6in)
10 Turret armour, 305 mm (12 in)
11 4.1 in AA guns (14)
12 Crane for aircraft
13 Bridge

Built Wilhelmshaven 1934-39
Weight 32,000 tons
Length 225 m (742 ft)
Beam 23.8 m (98 ft)
Draught 7.6 m (25 ft)
Crew 1900
Machinery Geared turbines, combined with Diesels. Three shafts
Design speed 27 kts
Top speed 32 kts
Aircraft 4 Arado
Total armour 12,517 tons

one failed to reach *Scharnhorst* complete. An aircraft had sent: 'Five warships, one apparently a big ship, NW of Norway.' Bey assumed that the sighting referred to his own destroyers. But the report was accurate. That 'big ship' was the Royal Navy's battleship *Duke of York*, with ten 14 in guns. With her was the cruiser *Jamaica*, the destroyers *Savage*, *Saumarez*, *Scorpion* and the Norwegian *Stord*.

Scharnhorst heads into a trap

The battle of North Cape began early on 26 December at 0825 when a destroyer signalled to *Scharnhorst*: 'Silhouette sighted four miles.' Thinking it was the convoy, Bey drove at full speed towards the scene—and into a trap. It was not the convoy. *Scharnhorst*'s first encounter with Burnett's cruisers led to her destruction. At 0922, *Belfast* signalled: 'Enemy in sight,' and

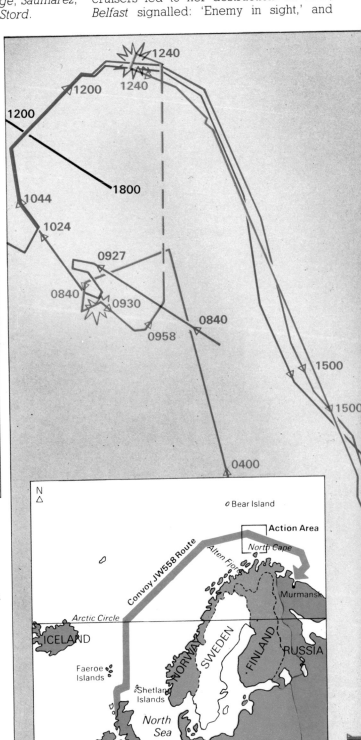

Top In her wartime dazzle camouflage, HMS *Belfast* steams out from Scapa Flow, the British fleet base in the Orkneys. This strange camouflage broke up the ship's silhouette and confused an enemy trying to plot her course or fix her position for torpedo or shell attack

Above HMS *Sheffield* makes smoke, normally a prohibited thing, for it can be seen for many miles by a searching enemy. But deliberate smoke could be created to lay an effective screen through which a surprise attack could be made

opened fire. In three minutes 8 in shells had hit *Scharnhorst*'s forward radar.

British radar was superior to the Germans'. *Norfolk* found the range in near-darkness, but the Germans had to use optical means and in the Arctic light very little could be seen. Only in daylight could the German ship exploit her superior firepower, so she broke off and headed north. Fraser then ordered destroyers to try to launch a torpedo attack to slow *Scharnhorst* down and let *Duke of York* in for the kill.

At 1220, after confused manoeuvres, *Sheffield* signalled: 'Enemy in sight'—Bey had not broken off the engagement, but had run into the cruiser screen. A gun duel began at ten kilometres (six miles). As the light had improved the German was no longer 'blind'   d her 11 in guns soon hit *Norfolk* and *Sheffield*.

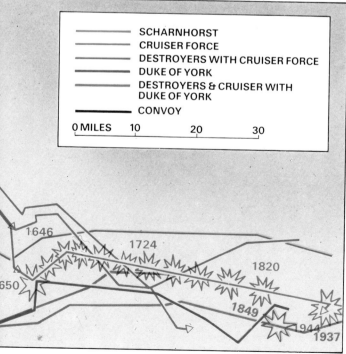

	SCHARNHORST
	CRUISER FORCE
	DESTROYERS WITH CRUISER FORCE
	DUKE OF YORK
	DESTROYERS & CRUISER WITH DUKE OF YORK
	CONVOY

0 MILES   10   20   30

Left Chart of the action off North Cape on 26 December 1943. The first clash came at 0400, followed by a gun-duel at 1240. *Scharnhorst* broke away but was later surrounded and destroyed. Of her crew of just under 2000 only 36 were rescued from the freezing, snow-swept sea. Not one officer was among them. Some days later, *Duke of York* steamed through the area and a guard of honour presented arms as a wreath was lowered into the sea

Above In happier days aboard the *Scharnhorst*, Vice-Admiral Otto Ciliax leads a crew inspection, followed at a respectful distance by the senior officers. Behind them the 11 in guns of the rear turret are plugged with tampions to preserve the rifling in the bores from salt corrosion. On top of the turret is the catapult for the ship's Arado spotter plane, which was badly damaged by shell splinters in the action and went down when the *Scharnhorst* sank

Bey's next move was strange, but he believed that *Duke of York* might be approaching, so he headed back towards Norway. *Scharnhorst*'s luck had now run out. The British battleship lay across her escape route, and with no forward radar the German could not spot her. In a burst of starshell, the German was illuminated, then she was obliterated by a 14 in salvo from *Duke of York*—each shell weighing 680 kg (1400 lb). It was the perfect straddle and possibly a hit. As *Scharnhorst* tried to escape she was hit again and again by the cruisers. Then *Duke of York*'s 14 in guns crippled the German's forward 11 in turret. At 1724 she signalled: 'Surrounded by a strong force,' but she still had teeth. The two battleships exchanged broadsides, two 11 in shells hitting the British vessel without exploding. The British ammunition was more reliable. As the German fled, the increase in range was an asset—the near vertical fall of British shell was more likely to penetrate the German's decks.

Bey's last message
Between 1830-1900 the turning point came as the German guns fell silent and her speed dropped. Then the destroyers closed in. Bey knew he had lost, sending a last message to Hitler: 'We shall fight to the last shell. Long live Germany and the Fuehrer. Scharnhorst onwards!'

The British battleships held their fire as the smaller ships moved in to 2750 metres (3000 yards), about five torpedoes striking home. Then the battleships opened fire again at 9.5 km (6 miles), silencing the last German guns. Desperately, she fired torpedoes at the British ships—all missed. Three more torpedoes exploded against her sides and the German crew were told to abandon ship.

Blazing from stem to stern, she settled by the bows. As she sank, Bey and his captain, Hintze, were standing calmly on the tilting bridge. *Scharnhorst* sank at about 1944. She had been struck by at least 11 torpedoes and 13 shells from *Duke of York*, with more of smaller calibre from the cruisers and destroyers. Of the German crew of 2000 only 36 were rescued from the freezing seas. Not one officer was found dead or alive. The last great gun duel between battleships had saved the Russian convoys and ended an era in naval warfare.

Ablaze from stem to stern, her turrets still futilely turned towards the enemy and guns trained for a final broadside, *Scharnhorst* begins to keel over. British destroyers close in on her starboard side to finish her off with their torpedoes

As 1943 ended the Russian front saw the route of the Wehrmacht as its haggard remnants straggled back towards their original starting point, the pre-war Polish frontier. The next year, 1944, began with Allied aircraft constantly battering at German industrial targets and repaying the carnage and havoc that the Luftwaffe had created over Rotterdam, many Belgian and French towns, Bristol, Coventry, Portsmouth, London and other British towns and cities.

But before June, there was still the Japanese threat to face. Japan's Burmese campaign had been largely repulsed, but the Nippon objective—Delhi—was still liable to come under attack if the Japanese 15th Army could succeed in destroying the British and Commonwealth forces in Burma.

While the battle for Imphal/Kohima was raging in the Far East, Germany was being hit night and day from the air. The RAFs heavy bombers attacked in force from the dark skies, and the US Eighth Air Force's Flying Fortresses in massed squadrons hit Luftwaffe airfields and armament factories by day. This softening up continued through the early, spring months of 1944 in preparation for the massive assault across the English Channel by the Allies.

When that day came to make the massive attack across the English Channel—to be forever known as D-Day—many of the officers in the German High Command knew that time was running out. The war could only go one way—and that in favour of the Allies.

The approach in those tossing landing craft to the smoke-shrouded Normandy beaches, the awareness that most pre-landing bombardments rarely eliminated a well-dug-in defence, and the constant roar of explosions on the beaches as known positions were blasted by shells from the Royal Navy and bombs from the free-ranging Allied air forces, was surely the most traumatic time of any soldier during World War 2.

Here, we outline the overall problems the Allies faced in getting across the Channel and on to the beaches; and the problems in estimating the depth and strength of the German divisions that would have to be overcome. Photographs of the complexes of concrete strongpoints dotted along the area were studied in 3-D to try to discover their weaknesses.

Our D-Day story concentrates on just one sector, called Omaha Beach. It was one of five beachheads involved in Operation Overlord. On Omaha, the softening-up bombardment, for all its smoke, fire and thunder, had been virtually useless and all the German soldiers had to do was check their gunsights and wait for the human targets to come into range.

An eastwards drift put soldiers on to beaches they did not recognize. Men died under intense cross-fire from machine-gun, small arms and mortar fire. But the set-back to the 5th Corps was finally overcome and the near-disaster turned into a firm beachhead from which the follow-up units could penetrate inland.

The third battle in this chapter concerns one that was planned five weeks after D-Day. The Allied advance had nearly ground to a halt. Something had to be done to penetrate farther into Occupied France, so midway through July Operation Goodwood was launched. It was not one of General Montgomery's most inspired battles, but it provided a corridor at Falaise through which the armour of General George S. Patton could break through into the heart of the German defences.

In Europe, the Battle of the Bulge had ended with the powerful German counter-attack being out-fought. It was here that the 6th SS Panzer Army and 7th Army created havoc and caused consternation at Allied High Command. But the Germans befouled their military reputation by massacring over 70 captured GIs at Malmedy. The German advance was finally halted at Celles on 25 December. Its story ends chapter 5.

Japanese hopes of a resounding victory in Burma seemed justified. An early Allied attempt to break the Japanese defences on the Donbiak Chaung had failed. It seemed that the Japanese would have to be destroyed rather than just driven back, and the man given the job was Lieutenant General Philip Christison, from 33rd Corps. He led 15th Corps with orders to clear the enemy from Arakan, in Burma. His aim was the destruction of the Japanese, not territorial gain.

During the first week of January, 161st Brigade probed the defences of the Rabazil network. Heavy shelling and bombing, supported by tanks, made little impact. After three days, heavy losses made Christison call it off. A switch was made to the eastern side of the Mayu Range, timed for 7 February.

But the Japanese moved first, Lieutenant General Tadashi Hanaya's Operation *Ha-Go* used 8000 men to strike at 114th Brigade on the east bank of the Kalapanzin to capture Taung Bazar, then swing left to destroy 7th Division. A smaller column would march north, left-wheel to cross the Mayu Range to block 5th Division's life-line—the Bawli Bazar-Maungdaw road.

The Japanese took suicidal risks on 3 February when a solid phalanx, 16 men abreast, marched down a 365 metre (400 yd) wide valley aware that 114th Brigade was in position on either side. But

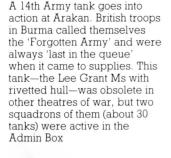

A 14th Army tank goes into action at Arakan. British troops in Burma called themselves the 'Forgotten Army' and were always 'last in the queue' when it came to supplies. This tank—the Lee Grant Ms with rivetted hull—was obsolete in other theatres of war, but two squadrons of them (about 30 tanks) were active in the Admin Box

the gamble paid off in the moonless night. The Brigade reported noises, but assumed they came from their own supply columns. Taken by surprise, the troops at Taung Bazar were wiped out.

'Hold the Admin Box!'

By 7 February, the Japanese were firmly astride the Ngakydeauk Pass, separating 5th and 7th Divisions. But the Sinzweya area—known as the Admin Box—was vital and had to be held at all costs.

Terrain advantage lay with the attackers. It was a clearing barely 1100 metres (1200 yd) in diameter, every inch covered by small-arms fire—a tactical trap. Dangerously close were piled ammunition dumps. The enemy could approach unseen right to the edge of the perimeter.

So cooks, storemen and muleteers prepared to defend the indefensible. Then a ragged group appeared from the jungle. They were stragglers from 7th Division HQ, which had been overrun that morning. The only orders were: 'Stay put and keep the Japanese out.' A few more men arrived, a Gurkha mortar battery a heavy AA troop, and two batteries of the 24th Mountain Regiment.

At midnight the first assault came. The muleteers showed exemplary discipline, holding their fire until the yelling Japanese were on top of them. They were repulsed. The next day Allied patrols were am-

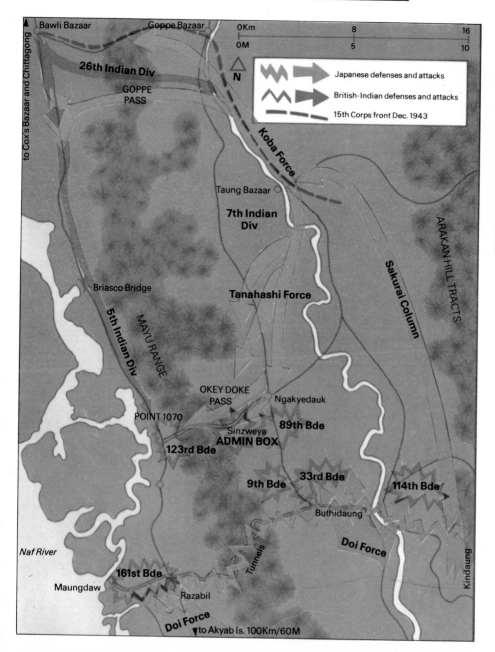

26th Indian Div

GOPPE PASS

Koba Force

Taung Bazaar

7th Indian Div

Briasco Bridge

5th Indian Div

MAYU RANGE

Tanahashi Force

Sakurai Column

ARAKAN HILL TRACTS

OKEY DOKE PASS

Ngakyedauk

POINT 1070

Sinzweya
89th Bde

123rd Bde

ADMIN BOX

9th Bde   33rd Bde

114th Bde

Buthidaung

Doi Force

Naf River

Tunnels

Kindaung

161st Bde

Maungdaw

Razabil

Doi Force

to Akyab Is. 100Km/60M

to Cox's Bazaar and Chittagong

Bawli Bazaar   Goppe Bazaar

0Km   8   16
0M   5   10

N

Japanese defenses and attacks
British-Indian defenses and attacks
15th Corps front Dec. 1943

Chittagong

Mandalay

Cox's Bazaar
Admin Box
Maungdaw

Foul Point
Akyab Island

ARAKAN YOMAS

Irrawaddy River

BAY OF BENGAL

Rangoon

0Km   150
0M   100

N

The large map shows the terrain around the Admin Box area, the positions of the British-Indian and Japanese defences. The detail map below shows how the Japanese virtually surrounded the Box, and every inch was within range of Japanese small-arms and MG fire

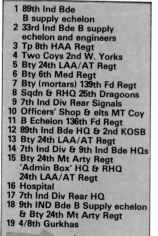

1 89th Ind Bde
   B supply echelon
2 33rd Ind Bde B supply
   echelon and engineers
3 Tp 8th HAA Regt
4 Two Coys 2nd W. Yorks
5 Bty 24th LAA/AT Regt
6 Bty 6th Med Regt
7 Bty (mortars) 139th Fd Regt
8 Sqdn & RHQ 25th Dragoons
9 7th Ind Div Rear Signals
10 Officers' Shop & elts MT Coy
11 B Echelon 136th Fd Regt
12 89th Ind Bde HQ & 2nd KOSB
13 Bty 24th LAA/AT Regt
14 7th Ind Div & 9th Ind Bde HQs
15 Bty 24th Mt Arty Regt
   'Admin Box' HQ & RHQ
   24th LAA/AT Regt
16 Hospital
17 7th Ind Div Rear HQ
18 9th IND Bde B Supply echelon
   & Bty 24th Mt Arty Regt
19 4/8th Gurkhas

Japanese attacks

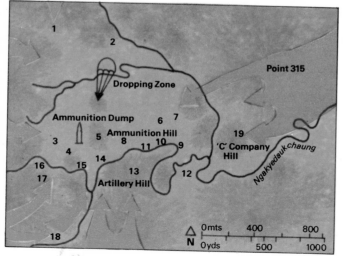

1

2

Point 315

Dropping Zone

Ammunition Dump

6   7

Ammunition Hill

19

'C' Company Hill

3   5
   8
4   11 10
14   9
   13   12
Artillery Hill

Ngakyedauk chaung

16
17
15

18

0mts   400   800
0yds   500   1000

N

Above The Japanese army on the march through difficult terrain were forced to wade leech-infested streams to avoid the known tracks

Left Guns had to be kept out of the cloying mud and makeshift plank bridges were constructed, slowing up their passage through deep jungle

This howitzer's 8.3 lb shell was no match for the armour of the Lee-Grant tank. **Muzzle velocity** 650 fps; **Traverse** 45°; **Range** 2312 m (3075 yd)

**MODEL 92 (1932)
70 MM HOWITZER (JAPANESE)**

bushed, and the Gurkhas were violently attacked and gave ground. The Japanese smashed through the perimeter and were halted by 37 mm and 75 mm tank guns.

In the early hours of the next day the Japanese infiltrated the Box hospital. They bayoneted the wounded on their stretchers then lined up six doctors and shot them. When counter-attacked, the Japanese used the survivors as shields as they retreated, killing them when they were safe.

Open sights and bayonets

At dawn on 9 February Japanese 70 mm howitzers opened up on the ammunition dumps. Fires were soon raging and crates of bullets and shells were exploding. The heavy AA troop engaged the Japanese guns over open sights and the surviving Japanese were bayoneted. Retribution came to the Japanese who had murdered the men in the hospital. An officer and 50 men were ambushed and killed.

By 11 February the first phase of the battle was over. The Japanese had failed to destroy 5th and 7th Divisions, not even throwing them into confusion. The Box, despite furious onslaughts, showed no signs of being swamped or running short of supplies.

Over the rest of the 7th Division area the three brigades had dug themselves in and though individually cut off were holding fast and hitting back hard.

Above Soldiers of the Royal Garhwal Rifles on reconnaissance patrol in the broken jungle of Arakan

Left This is the clearing in Admin Box as seen from Ammunition Hill. Brigadier Evans was under orders to hold this clearing to the bitter end. Defence was very difficult; only 1097 m (1200 yd) across it was all within rifle range

Below Men of the Tripura Rifles lie in ambush in the Arakan jungle, ready to surprise a Japanese patrol with a hail of bullets

Bottom Italian troops of the Mahrattas form up in preparation for an attack on a Japanese-occupied position. These operations were the most gruelling and exhausting actions, carried out in very hot and humid conditions

A major Japanese attack was directed at Artillery Hill, a bare 180 m (200 yd) from HQ. Hidden by the jungle, the enemy advanced to within yards of the gunners and their first charge swamped the position.

Then a plan for infantry/tank co-operation proved brilliantly successful. As the infantry counter-attacked, the tanks saturated their objective with HE until the infantry commander fired a Very light. It was the signal for the AFVs to switch to solid shot. The enemy were still forced to keep their heads down until the leading section was about 14 m (15 yd) from their line. Then they charged with bayonet and grenade before the stunned Japanese could react.

Artillery Hill was retaken. After ten days not one of the Box's positions had fallen. But casualties were mounting.

Outside the Box there were setbacks. The key to the Ngakyedauk Pass, Point 1070, was overrun, but the relief of the Box could only be a matter of hours. But during the night troops were subjected to continual *kamikaze* attacks and hurled back, leaving the position in enemy hands.

By the 19th, general conditions were deteriorating. The hospital was a shambles as the wounded piled up. Ammunition was short as dumps were hit. Then on 21 February Point 1070 was taken. This successful assault opened the way to the Box and 123rd Brigade moved down the Pass, mopping up isolated Japanese.

Forced to admit failure, Hanaya was obliged to cancel *Ha-Go* as 7th Division's brigades fanned out to cut off Sakuri's withdrawal. But the ordeal of Admin Box was not quite over. On 21-22 February the Japanese broke through to within 19 m (20 yd) of 9th Brigade HQ, their suicidal charge coming near to succeeding. But they were driven off, leaving 30 dead.

Hanaya's Ha-Go disaster

On 24 February the last Japanese had been driven from the immediate neighbourhood of the Pass. For Hanaya, the failure of *Ha-Go* was a disaster. Out of Sakuri's picked 8000, fewer than 3000 starving, exhausted Japanese fought their way back. He had neither failed to destroy 15th Corps nor pinned down 14th Army's reserves. The defeat of *Ha-Go* was one of the turning points of World War 2. For the first time, the Japanese had suffered a major defeat on land at British-Indian hands.

The Allied invasion of German-held France was fixed for 6 June along 65 km (40 miles) of the Normandy coast. General Montgomery had selected 21st Army Group, of six reinforced infantry divisions landing from the sea and three airborne divisions. Five beachheads were selected: on the west, Utah and Omaha for the US 1st Army and on the west, Gold, Juno and Sword for the British 2nd Army. On the German side, an invasion had been expected, but there were rarely more than 25 full-strength field divisions at readiness.

This is the story of the near disaster at Omaha beach, where the US 5th Corps were to land. Their task was to gain an adequate foothold within two hours and then clear the exits. The day's objective was to advance 6 km (4 miles) inland and secure the plateau to the river Aure.

So, at 0300, 34,000 men and 3300 vehicles in 300 landing craft pitched and tossed in a heavy sea as they circled into formation. The sea took its toll as 32 'amphibious' tanks sank, an artillery battalion lost all but one of its guns as amphibious vehicles foundered, 300 fully armed soldiers were thrown into the rough seas as their landing craft sank.

At Omaha, with 40 minutes to go before they hit the beach, the massive sea and air bombardment of the defences reached its ear-splitting climax as 500 US Air Force bombers rained bombs down, with 3500 shells from battleships.

As the landing craft nosed towards the beach the softening-up bombardment ceased. It was a silent prelude to disaster. Not one bomb had fallen on the defences and the naval shelling had overshot too. A strong lateral drift had taken the landing craft well away from their planned areas.

Wrong beach—wrong time

Then the German batteries opened up. Artillery, mortars, machine-guns smashed into the 6 km (4 mile) Omaha beach as the landing craft disembarked their soldiers. Confusion followed as men waded on to the wrong beach at the wrong time. The special Engineer Task Force, whose job was to

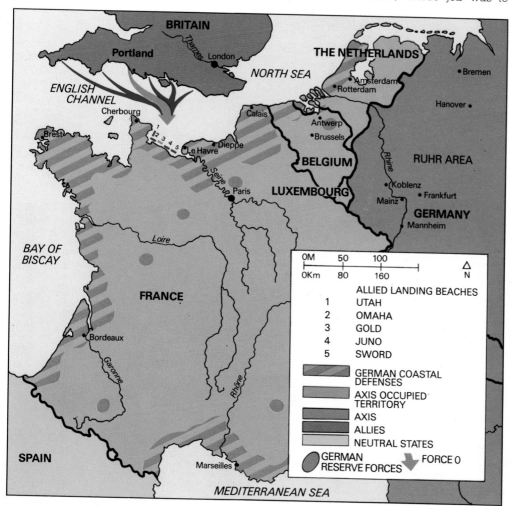

The southern coast of England, with the take-off points for the invasion of Normandy on D-Day, 6 June 1944. The five Normandy beaches are shown with the courses taken by the Allied assault force. Of little hindrance was the much-vaunted Atlantic Wall, which turned out to be partly finished

Below The ramps crash down at Omaha Beach, for many soldiers the last sound they heard. The troops of the 1st US Infantry Division splash desperately ashore seeking cover that was not there and the German defences were about to take terrible toll

Bottom The defences that faced the assault troops

clear gaps through the many obstacles erected on the beaches, lost 50 percent of its number. But six lanes were cut through the defences before the incoming tide submerged them, not enough for the follow-up waves of infantry, who suffered heavy casualties in the increasing confusion. Few craft got their soldiers off with dry feet, many GIs stepping into water neck deep.

All along Utah beach casualties were heavy. The 2nd Ranger Battalion suffered severely. One of their two landing craft was sunk before it reached the beach, the other was shredded by machine-gun fire as the ramp went down, only 12 men out of 65 got 180 m (200 yd) from the beach alive. Most died as they ran down the ramp.

At 0700, a second group of five follow-up waves beached. None found the conditions they expected. The first waves had not got beyond the sea wall, none of the known defences had been neutralized. These men

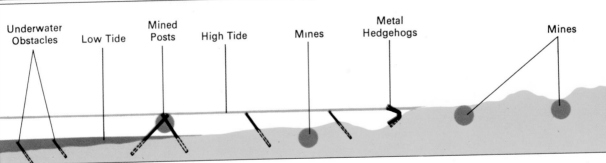

Underwater Obstacles   Low Tide   Mined Posts   High Tide   Mines   Metal Hedgehogs   Mines

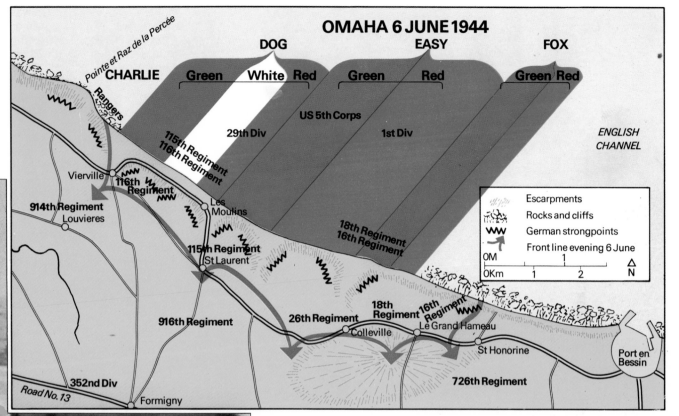

OMAHA 6 JUNE 1944

DOG EASY FOX

CHARLIE | Green White Red | Green Red | Green Red

Rangers

Pointe et Raz de la Percée

US 5th Corps

29th Div

ENGLISH
CHANNEL

1st Div

Vierville

116th Regiment

914th Regiment
Louvieres

115th Regiment
116th Regiment

116th
Regiment

Les
Moulins

115th Regiment
St Laurent

18th Regiment
16th Regiment

	Escarpments
	Rocks and cliffs
ᴡᴡ	German strongpoints
	Front line evening 6 June

0M   1
0Km   1   2   N

916th Regiment

26th Regiment

18th
Regiment
Colleville

16th
Regiment
Le Grand Hameau

St Honorine

Port en
Bessin

352nd Div

Road No. 13

Formigny

726th Regiment

had not trained for frontal assault; their task was to mop up any by-passed pockets of resistance. But all they saw was the carnage on the beaches, debris and bodies bobbing among wrecked landing craft. Groups of silent, shocked and wounded men sat in the desolation. Machine-gun fire continued to rip into GIs trying to get inland from the beach. To stay was inviting death, to move was to bring a hail of bullets.

The German defences had not been reduced, although slowly men managed to get to fighting positions. The second assault group had not suffered the dire casualties of the first. But still the cruel defensive fire swamped the approaching landing craft, and when the survivors reached the beach ahead of them lay the enemy, minefields and booby-trapped wire.

The situation looked critical, the beaches were choked with men and vehicles which by now should have penetrated inland. Further landings would have to wait until the exits were cleared.

GIs advance at last

Then heroism, desperation and leadership forged groups of men into fighting units who started to move forward, supported by the few remaining tanks. Advances were made amid smoke and confusion. An impetus developed as the enemy fire slackened under the pressure.

Above The Omaha D-Day objective was Road No. 13. It took six hours to fight through the beach defences and by the close of the day 17 US battalions had got just 2.4 km (1.5 miles) inland through five German defences. Finally, 34,000 men were got ashore to form a beachhead alongside the rest of the huge Allied force

The leading infantry were joined by units and together they got to high ground. Suddenly they found the enemy had left their forward defences. By 0830 the invasion had made 275 m (300 yd) and the last groups of infantry were moving in from the sea wall where they had been pinned down. The bridgehead expanded slowly and the beaches were cleared.

Either side, the British 2nd Army had broken through, and to the west the American 7th Corps was firmly ashore, with men and materials pouring in.

At the end of that cruel day, 5th Corps had two firm footholds on Omaha beach, but nowhere more than 1.5 km (1 mile) deep. The cost had been 2000 killed, 50 tanks and 25 guns destroyed.

Omaha is a story of near disaster but no shame. Unseasoned troops subjected to a complex amphibious operation, compounded by bad weather and stubborn opposition, were initially paralysed by shock, but they rallied and resumed a dogged offensive. The Allies were back on French soil and the Germans falling back.

Above A corporal of the US 101st Airborne Division. He dropped behind Utah beach on D-Day

Above right the 1st Infantry Division comes ashore as a smoke-screen drifts along Omaha beach. The water was deep, with men wading up to their necks

Right US infantry carrying MGs and demolition charges in satchels. They were part of the second assault wave and made their way past bodies and items of discarded equipment

Above The Germans were waiting behind the pre-assault barrage, the smoke of which can be seen. Lying close to hand is a stick grenade and an MG ready for when the invading troops come into range

Left The invasion at last begins to make ground. Following the decimated first waves, back-up troops in amphibious vehicles and halftracks, towing 57 mm AT guns, splash out of the water to cross the debris-littered beach. The main danger at this point was from artillery and mortar fire

OPERATION GOODWOOD

By the fifth week after D-Day it seemed that the battle for Normandy had congealed like the Western Front in World War 1. The British and Canadians had waged a long-drawn-out struggle for Caen, while the Americans fought bitter battles in the bocage of the west flank, suffering 40,000 casualties. Although Caen had fallen on 10 July, progress in the British sector seemed small. East of the Orne, 1st British Corps faced obstinately-held defences of great strength. At Caen, 2nd Canadian Corps controlled only the northern half of the city, the industrial Vaucelles had still to fall.

On 10 July General Montgomery conferred with his two commanders, the American Lieutenant General Omar Bradley, and Lieutenant General Sir Miles Dempsey. The enemy's armour was to be drawn into battle on the eastern flank and kept there so the Americans could break out and exploit their superior mobility in the open country south of Avranches. Obviously, German infantry reinforcements were beginning to arrive to relieve the armour on the British front and the formidable *Panzer Lehr* Division had arrived on the US front.

Right An RAF B25 Mitchell medium bomber attacks a Colombelles factory by the River Orne

Far right British tanks roll across a Bailey bridge over the Caen ship canal. There were six of these military-built bridges

Right Defensive slit trenches dug by British troops before the attack on the Odon Valley. Some keep careful watch while others get some much-needed rest

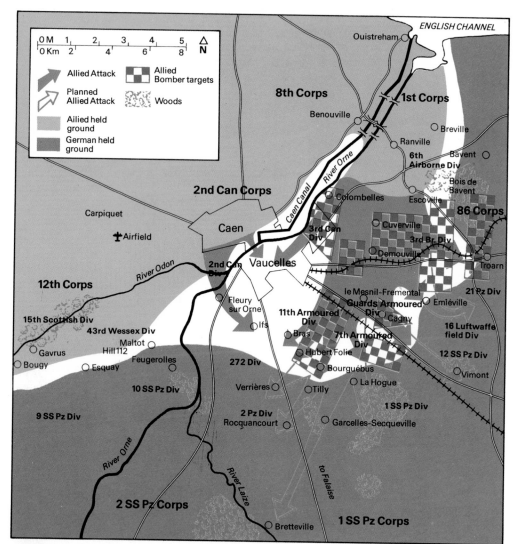

Left Battle map of the three-day Goodwood offensive. The 'Racing' code-name was deliberate; the tanks lined up at a starting post and rushed down the prelaid bombed target until the finish line. At least, that was the plan, but German AT guns held out to hold the British until Panzer reserves could be brought forward

Below Taking the village of Cagny became difficult, with the Germans holding on doggedly. Twelve Sherman tanks were destroyed here. A dispatch rider waits for his final orders

'Strike south from Caen'

Montgomery ordered Dempsey to strike south from Caen with a strong armoured force east of the Orme between Caen and Falaise, calling it Operation Goodwood. Meanwhile, Bradley was to continue his advance to Avranches, break out, swing right south of the bocage towards Le Mans and Alencon to envelope the rear of both Seventh Army and *Panzergruppe West*. The new offensive would start on 18 July, using three armoured divisions from the airborne bridgehead east of Caen and the Orme, the US First Army mounting a heavy attack at St Lo the next day.

The main objectives would be limited to the ground south of Caen, with no intention of establishing a division 30 km (20 miles) south of Falaise. The aims of 8th Corps were to engage German armour in battle, wipe it out and get a good bridgehead over the Orme and kill as many Germans as possible. On 16 and 17 July the Canadians were to create the impression that the main attack would come west of the Orme. Bailey bridges were built over the Orme and the Canal de Caen, but the Germans were watching from chimneys in Colombelles.

General Hans Eberbach had exploited the situation, convinced that the British would attack, if only because they had failed to break out elsewhere; his Intelligence on 15 July read: 'British are planning major operation across the Orme towards the south-east about 17 July.' On this front were 86 Corps, and two armoured divisions with Tiger tanks.

So British 8th Corps faced a determined enemy in a very strong defensive position. Montgomery's concept seemed simple enough, but it bristled with difficulties. Under German observation, the armoured divisions would have to enter the battle one at a time; the supporting artillery would have to stay west of the Orme. A nightmare traffic problem loomed.

Eighth Corps were about to attack where everything was in the enemy's favour, and 4500 Allied aircraft were necessary to redress the balance. The night of 17-18 July was hot and dark. Soon after 0100, 11th Armoured Division started to cross the bridges, heading for the forming-up area east of Ranville. As dawn broke, the bombers appeared. Guided by pathfinders, they released their bombs. A huge

No weapon was too vicious to use in the fighting across France after the invasion. Here a Canadian carrier has been equipped with Wasp flame-throwing gear, leaving a path of blazing debris in its wake

Left Accurate and punishing mortar fire often slowed down the Allied advance and British troops here are forced to take scant cover in ditches and banks

Bottom left Much of the success of the Allied operation was due to superior air cover. Here are items of German armour knocked out by rocket-firing Typhoons. The tank in the foreground has been coated with an anti-magnetic mine cement, but it was no match for the destructive power of the rockets

SHERMAN VC FIREFLY

Crew 4
Weight 34.75 tons
Max speed
(Roads): 35 k/h (22 mph)
(Rough ground): 16 k/h (10 mph)
Range
(Roads): 201 k/h (125 miles)
(Rough ground): 30.4 km (50 miles)
Length 7.3 m (25 ft 6 in)
Width 2.3 m (9 ft 6 in)
Height 2.3 m (9 ft 4 in)
Engine 1 Chrysler A57 30-cylinder (five units of 6 cylinders)
Armament One 17-pounder 76.2 mm Mk IV gun with 78 rounds
One .30 Browning MG
One .50 Browning MG
Armour Front hull: 51 mm
Sides: 38 mm (1.5 in)
Rear: 38 mm (1.5 in)
Top: 19 mm (0.8 in)
Turret: Front: 76 mm (3 in)
Sides: 51 mm (2 in)
Rear: 51 mm (2 in)
Top: 25 mm (1 in)

The Sherman Firefly tank was at that stage of the war one of the most effective AFVs in the Allies' armoury.

Above Savage street fighting gave no quarter either side. Here, Canadians work their way through a street house-by-house

Below A scene reminiscent of World War 1. Most of the French village of Cagny was devastated by shellfire and bombing, but tank rounds punish small buildings too. A British salvage crew is recovering a damaged Sherman

cloud of smoke and dust began to form as 2500 tons of bombs fell on Colombelles and 650 tons on Cagny.

Then 15 in naval guns saturated all known enemy battery positions. More fighter-bombers and heavy bombers arrived at 0700. Altogether, 7000 tons of bombs had pulverized an area less than 26 km (10 miles) square.

Stunned and paralysed by bombing

At H-Hour, 0745, 11th Armoured Division plunged forwards into the dust and smoke. First objective was Le Mesnil-Frementel, 5 km (3 miles) from the start line. At first they had an easy run. The enemy were stunned and paralysed by the bombing. By 0900 the AFVs had passed artillery cover. But soon

the Germans started to recover as 88s knocked out 12 Shermans. Farther west the Canadians were meeting resistance. Determined to put up a defence the Germans flung 21st Panzer Division against the Guards and 11th Armoured. A storm of AP shot stopped tanks of the 3rd RTR at Bras. Then Panthers arrived to mop up survivors, but the British held their ground. The battle's confusion defied all efforts by commanders to conduct it. Only darkness could call a halt and restore coherence.

At last, at 1800, 2nd Armoured secured a footing in ruined Cagny. On the right, 3rd Canadians had entered Colombelles; 3rd British Division had reached the outskirts of Troarn. Montgomery had extended his bridgehead at the cost of 1500 casualties and 200 AFVs. This was all he had to show for the greatest air support and largest tank attack of the war.

Disappointing it might have been for the Allies, it was more depressing for the Germans. They had failed to drive the British back across the Caen-Troarn line and had lost 109 AFVs. At dawn next morning the advance continued. About 1600, 11th Armoured attacked and wiped out an infantry battalion of 1st SS Panzer Division. The German Command had now decided that their men were nearing the limit of endurance and could only hold on until reinforcements arrived. Then a violent rainstorm struck, continuing for 48 hours and the front was a sea of mud. Both sides had fought to a standstill. Goodwood ended in disillusion, discomfort and anticlimax.

Goodwood was the least inspired of Montgomery's battles, but strategically it was a great victory. Six Panzer Divisions had been drawn to the eastern flank, making room for General Patton to penetrate through the Falaise Gap on 25 July.

The war was drawing to a long-overdue close as 1945 began. In their hearts the German and Japanese leaders knew that the sands had run out for them. Hitler, with the blinkered vision of the fanatic, would never accept it. He chose to throw the remnants of the Luftwaffe against the now-overwhelming numbers of Allied aircraft that occupied the skies over Germany, bringing death and destruction to the Fatherland, the very thing that Hitler had promised the German people would never happen. That the German fighters were not only outnumbered but terminally short of fuel and ammunition as well as trained pilots, powerless to make nothing more than token resistance, was beyond his understanding. He could not accept the truth.

So as New Year's Day 1945 dawned, as many FW190s and other Luftwaffe fighters as could be mustered were launched against the rampaging Allied bombers and fighterbombers. The predictable outcome, in an air-battle called Bodenplatte ('Baseplate'), is told first in this chapter. It was the end of Goering's Luftwaffe as an effective fighting force.

In the Pacific, on 15 February, a set-piece battle took place when Iwo Jima was the scene of yet more scenes of bloody hand-to-hand combat. Only 216 Japanese survived out of the garrison of 23,000 soldiers when the struggle in the black, powdery lava beaches came to an end.

Iwo Jima typifies the bloody and unremitting assault by American forces on the Japanese-held islands in the Pacific. The same kind of fighting was repeated many times and in every case each Japanese defender had to be eliminated. There were virtually no mass surrenders even when their position was obviously untenable. The Japanese military code prevented any surrender, an action which demeaned the soldier in the face of his peers and, worse, in the eyes of his ancestors.

In Europe, the war was now on German soil and its civilian population was suffering. The time had come for desperate measures. Field Marshal Kesselring had gained a well-earned reputation in the past four years as a successful leader, but his defences were now too weak to stop Generals Patten and Montgomery, whose soldiers had the initiative and military backup to press on into the heart of Germany.

After crossing the Rhine, the Allies began to move along the Ruhr Valley. By April 17, over 317,000 German soldiers had surrendered. This number did not, however, include Field Marshal Model, who shot himself rather than face the POW cage and retribution when the final account was paid.

Soon Berlin itself was under siege and by the enemy the Germans feared most—the Red Army. The German civilian feared it because he knew of the Russians' brutal treatment of captured German soldiers; but the Wehrmacht feared the Russians because they also knew of the dreadful atrocities carried out by them as they were first invading and then retreating from Russian soil. There would be little mercy shown by the Red Army when it reached Berlin.

With the rape of the German capital, the war in Europe was virtually over, but in the Pacific the Japanese were preparing themselves to fight to the last man, woman and child. Hiroshima and Nagasaki were to be the funeral pyres of the Japanese, pyres which saved untold Allied lives in the long run. The first atomic bombs brought Japan to its knees and ended World War 2.

We do not yet know whether these bombs, the 20 kilotonne 'Little Boy' and 'Fat Man', heralded the eventual destruction of mankind in a nuclear holocaust, or showed the world that if we must have war it must not be fought with those horrific weapons.

BODENPLATTE

In the first faint light of New Year's Day 1945 30 German fighter aircraft began to move slowly out of their dispersal pens and on to the snow-covered taxi-track. Black-overalled ground crew hunched their shoulders, cursing, as the propeller-wash blew clouds of snow into the air. FW190D-9 'Doras' stood on spindly, stork-like under-carriages. Then the squadron jockeyed awkwardly for take-off position and the engines howled up to full power, and two by two the slim fighters gathered speed down the runway.

Shortly after 0800 all 30 Focke-Wulfs were airborne, and in loose formations they turned westwards and followed *Hauptmann* Hrdlicka towards the assembly area above Koblenz. *I Gruppe Jagdgeschwader 2 'Richthofen' (I/JG2)* was off to war again.

With so pitifully few flying hours in their log-books the young pilots could hardly manage simple take-offs and landings in perfect conditions; one or two could not disguise the fact that they were actually frightened by their big, demanding aircraft. In this winter of 1944-45 they had precious little opportunity to find their confidence and their first easy kill under experienced flight commanders. There were no easy kills for anyone any more . . . not with the skies black with Spitfires and Tempests, and huge formations of Mustangs and Thunderbolts ranging over the western *Reich* at will.

Perhaps this mission would earn a breath-ing space in which the teenage pilots could at least learn the rudiments of air combat before facing the swarming enemy once again. Perhaps, after today, a few of them would live long enough for their ground crews to learn their names and faces, before they disappeared forever . . . for it was no ordinary squadron mission, on this first day of 1945.

Flown at tree-top height

The idea of a single great blow at the Allied tactical air forces on the Continent, a mass fighter and fighter-bomber attack at first light, launched with complete secrecy and flown at tree-top height, was an integral part of the planning for Hitler's last great offensive in the West, the Panzer thrust through the Ardennes. A superhuman effort was made during October-December 1944 to build up the strength of the Fighter Arm and preserve it for a co-ordinated raid. Somehow a total of 1000 fighters and nearly 400 ground-attack machines were made ready by mid-December. Their mission was to be two-fold: first, the co-ordinated strike at Allied airfields, to negate the enormous advantage of air superiority enjoyed by the Allies since D-Day; and when that had been achieved, the direct support of the Panzer divisions in their advance.

On 14 December 1944 *Geschwader* and *Gruppe* commanders were summoned to *Jagdkorps II* HQ near Altenkirchen east of Bonn for a briefing by the plan's architect, *Generalmajor* Dietrich Peltz. The strike was codenamed *Bodenplatte* ('Baseplate'). On 16 December the ground offensive opened —but without Bodenplatte.

Right Oberstleutnant (Lt. Col.) Heinz Bar led *JG3* in the successful raid on Eindhoven. This pilot had already made 202 kills in Africa, Russia and the West. He wears the Knight's Cross with oakleaves and swords, a high German military honour

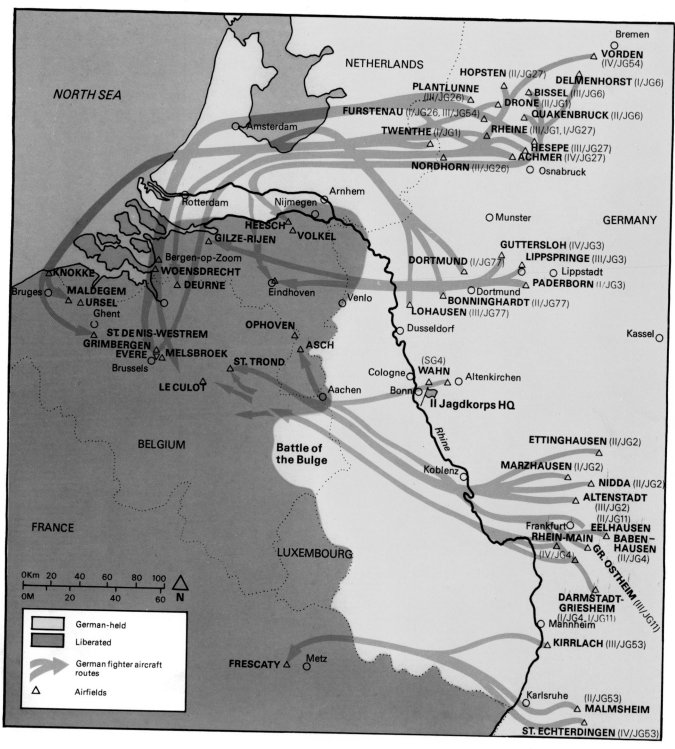

The poor visibility which kept Allied aircraft on the ground during the initial phases of the Battle of the Bulge also grounded the Luftwaffe. The immediate requirements of tactical support and of fending off intense Allied pressure on their own airfields fully occupied the Luftwaffe when the weather began to lift on Christmas Eve. In the final week of December air fighting was extremely heavy, particularly on the 29th. The Luftwaffe lost 535 fighter pilots dead, captured, or missing and 194 more wounded during the month, so the German commanders were astonished when they heard on 31 December that the operation they had thought 'shelved' was to be carried out the following morning.

The depth of the briefing given to the actual squadron aircrew varied from unit to unit. It seems that only *Staffelkapitäne* (Flight

The last concentrated Luftwaffe operation of the war used 930 of its fighters against 18 Allied forward airfields. Five were attacked by mistake. Germany probably lost 300 machines to the Allies' 400, but the reserves of the Allies were far greater and were replaced immediately

FOCKE-WULF 190D-9 (*JG26*)

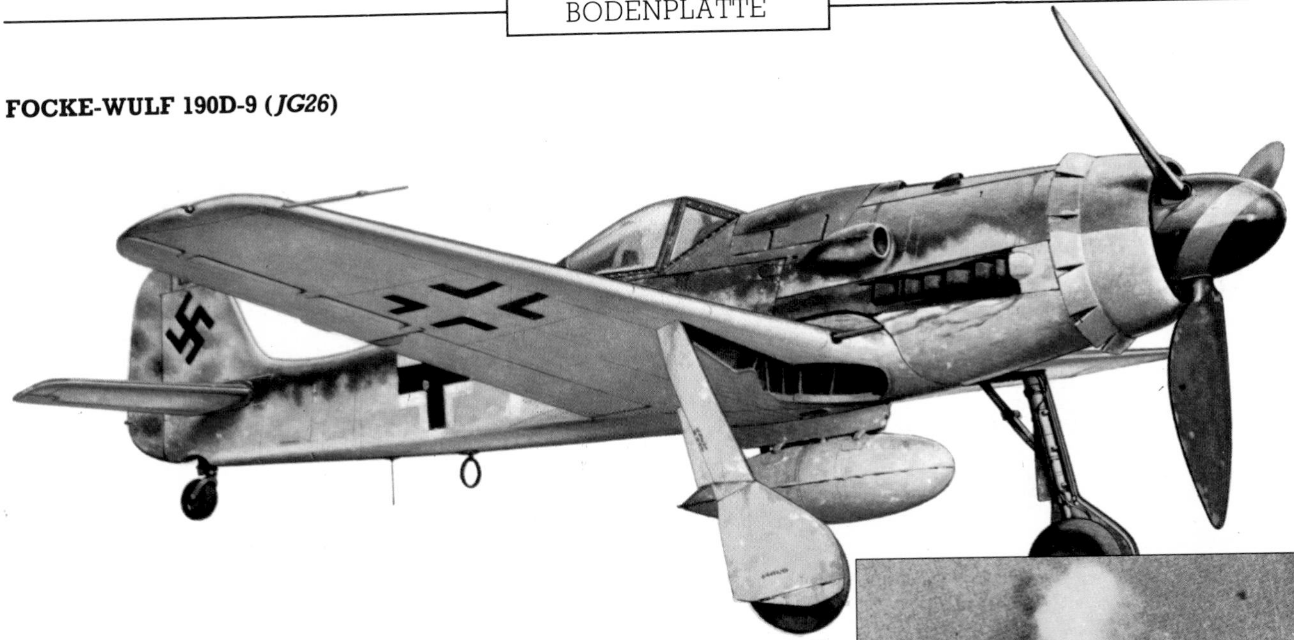

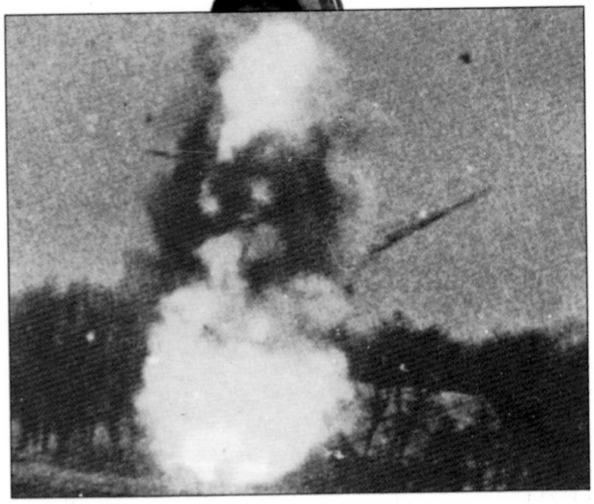

Right An FW190 explodes as it is hit by rounds from a US fighter. This was the fate of 57 of the Bodenplatte raiders

Leaders) were let into the secret on 31 December, the other pilots not being briefed until well before dawn on the morning of the 1st.

Many of the younger and less experienced pilots were unequal to the task of navigating themselves around the Low Countries, as their training was appallingly sketchy. Largely for their benefit each attacking force would be led by two night-fighter Ju88s or 188s until close to the target. In all, no fewer than 33 fighter and one ground-attack *Gruppen* belonging to 12 *Geschwadern* would take part. Every aircraft carried a 245 litre (65 gallon) jettison-fuel tank as many of the targets were at extreme range. Post-war German estimates of fighter strength involved in Bodenplatte put the total at rather over 900 aircraft.

By 0800 most of the attacking squadrons were airborne in moderate to good visibility; there was heavier cloud cover over the Dutch-Belgian border, as forecast. Flying at between 15 m (50 ft) and 45 m (150 ft) behind their twin-engined pathfinders, the Me109s and FW190s headed for their targets. *JGs 1, 6, 26* and *27*, with half of *JG54*, were to fly from their bases in north-west Germany in a series of dog-legs west and south, to fall upon the three Brussels airfields, Volkel and St Denis-Westrem.

From fields to the north-east of Dortmund *JG3* would strike almost due west at Eindhoven. From north-east of Cologne, *JG77* would fly a great multiple dog-leg north, west and south and strike at Antwerp-Deurne from the north. There was to be a mid-air rendezvous between *JG2* from north of Frankfurt, III *Gruppe, Schlachtgeschwader 4* from around Cologne and Bonn. Together its FW190F-8 fighter bombers and *JG2*'s Focke-Wulfs and Me109Gs and Ks would hit St Trond. From the complex of airstrips south of Frankfurt *JG4* and *JG11* would strike north-west at Le Culot and Asch respectively. Finally, far to the south, *JG53 'Pik-As'* would fly from its airfields around Karlsruhe to attack Metz-Frescaty in France.

The attacks were due to take place virtually simultaneously, at around 0920 in the morning. By noon the same day the Luftwaffe fighters would be back on their bases, having destroyed Allied air superiority over Western Europe. That was the theory, but that was all it was.

Below When the Luftwaffe planes got through they did effective damage. Here two petrol bowsers blaze after their tanks were punctured by bullets

An appalling butcher's bill

By noon, some had indeed arrived back at base. They left behind them 18 *Geschwader*, *Gruppe* and *Staffel* commanders and 197 other pilots dead, captured, or missing; the fate of 48 of these latter is still unknown. Of those who regained German lines 18 were wounded. Against this appalling butcher's bill of aircrew the Luftwaffe could set not the destruction of Allied air power, nor even its crippling, but merely a temporary pause in certain types of operation, made good within a matter of days. German claims and admitted Allied losses on 1 January 1945 vary between the German claim of 479 enemy aircraft destroyed and 114 damaged, and the British (US figures in brackets) record of 144 (134) destroyed and 84 (62) damaged. RAF losses totalled 40 officers and men dead and 145 wounded on the ground, and six pilots shot down. US losses were considerably lighter.

The ability of 2nd Tactical Air Force and 9th USAAF to prosecute the war over Germany's western frontiers was reduced on a purely local and temporary level, and the strain on squadrons which remained operational increased severely for a week or so. But damage inflicted was strategically insignificant.

Successful attacks were made on Eindhoven and Brussels-Evère. The former was the target for *JG3 'Udet'* which mustered some 70 fighters—two *Gruppen* of Me109s and one of FW190As. Led by *Oberstleutnant* Heinz Bär, *JG3* took off at 0830. The Wing formed over Lippstadt and headed west on its 225 km (140 mile) flight in a spread-out formation. Crossing the Rhine, they penetrated the Dutch frontier 24 km (15 miles) north of Venlo; in the final stage they swung right around Eindhoven to hit the airfield from the south-west. A few split away to attack Gilze-Rijen while the main force worked over Eindhoven, the home of eight Typhoon and three Spitfire squadrons. Two of the former were airborne and another was about to take off as *JG3* made its first strafing run. Several RAF fighters were shot down as they lifted off; others managed to scramble into the middle of the raid and inflict casualties. The perimeter AA brought down some of the attackers, but fires were started at several points and many aircraft were shot up.

After the attack No. 438 (Typhoon) Squadron reported only two untouched aircraft; No. 440 had all but two destroyed, and those that survived badly hit; and 124 Wing's four squadrons could muster only 24

Above Polish fighter pilots were ever keen to get at the Luftwaffe. Here, three Spitfire IXs of No. 308 Krakowski (City of Cracow) Polish Fighter Squadron RAF take-off from Grimbergen, near Brussels, after its home base at St Denis-Westrem was put out of action

Left Allied aircraft burn after being strafed by German fighters. A Stirling transport and Spitfire IXs are wrecked, but 18 FW190 attackers were shot down

aircraft between them. Nine Spitfires of No. 400 Squadron suffered as well, and in all 25 pilots were killed. After 20 minutes *JG3* split up into small elements and headed home. They suffered casualties from Allied fighters on the return flight. Total pilot losses were ten killed and six captured, with two wounded as against at least 50 Allied aircraft destroyed.

At Brussels-Evère the 'long-noses' of *II/JG26 Schlageter* and the Me109Gs and Ks of *III Gruppe*, led by *Major* Hackl and

Trigger-happy German defences

By contrast the attempt on Maldegem and St Denis-Westrem by *JG1 'Oesau'* provides a perfect example of all that went wrong with Bodenplatte. *I* and *III Gruppen* (55 fighters) were targeted on to Maldegem, about 16 km (ten miles) east of Bruges, which they would attack from a seaward direction after a short flight guided by two Ju88s. The trouble started when German flak brought down three aircraft of *I/JG1*. Supposedly briefed, German AA defences along the

FOCKE-WULF 190A-8

Weight 9,660 lb; **Engine** BMW 801D2 air cooled, 1700 hp; **Guns** 2×13 mm MG, 4×20 mm cannon; **Speed** 655 km/h (408 mph) at 6300 m (20,670 ft); **Range** 793 km (497 miles). *Bodenplatte* employed 231 A-8s

Hauptmann Walther Krupinski, caught Spitfires of 127 (Canadian) Wing in the process of taxying out for take off when they attacked at 0920. The two strong *Gruppen*, mustering about 100 aircraft between them, made between ten and 15 strafing runs and destroyed many aircraft; hangars and fuel bowsers were set on fire, and the AA defences comprehensively worked over. While *JG26*'s claim of 120 aircraft destroyed was probably optimistic, the *Geschwader* undoubtedly put paid to many times its own seven dead or missing and five captured.

whole front proved understandably trigger-happy throughout the morning. It is estimated that no fewer than 100 of the German losses in Bodenplatte were due to German ground fire.

At Maldegem, *JG1* got into a chaotic state. Five FW190A-8s departed to check out a satellite airstrip nearby. Five strafing runs had been planned, but the pilots of *I/* and *III/JG1* only made one or two runs, finding it hard to spot targets and just spraying the area generally. They suffered further losses on their return, losing 13 pilots, including two commanders. At Maldegem they had destroyed 11 Spitfires of No. 485 (New Zealand) Squadron and damaged two others.

At St Denis-Westrem the 25 FW190A-8s of *II/JG1* found that all three Polish squadrons of 131 Wing RAF were already airborne. No. 302 Squadron was just landing, and ran into a hail of German cannot-fire and the British AA barrage; ten Spitfires were destroyed. The other Polish squadrons were recalled immediately, and dog-fights took place over Ghent, so the final *II Gruppe* toll of 18 Spitfires and two pilots had to be set against 11 German pilots killed, captured and missing and one wounded. The total *Geschwader* score was thought to be 32 Spitfires and two pilots, against 24 German pilots who failed to return, a loss rate of 31 per cent for *JG1*.

At St Trond the pilots of *JG2* and *SG4*, already thinned out by their own and Allied flak, found the P47 Thunderbolts and the ground defences of 48th and 404th Fighter Groups (9th USAAF) already alerted by signals from airborne comrades. The four *Gruppen* ran into a hail of fire, and only managed to destroy a small number of aircraft. The *'Richthofen'* Wing lost 33 pilots dead, missing and captured; *I Gruppe*, from Merzhausen on the snowy northern slopes of the Taunus, lost 16. *III/SG4* lost four pilots to 'friendly' flak, including *Geschwader Kommodore*, *Obersleutnant* Alfred Druschel.

Jagdgeschwader 4 never even found Le Culot. Some of them hit St Trond, already stirred up by the attacks of *JG2* and *SG4*, and suffered accordingly. The unit became hopelessly split up, with individual *Staffeln* roaming the Low Countries shooting up targets of opportunity on the roads and suffering heavily from Allied flak. For such paltry results *JG4* sacrificed 25 machines, and 23 pilots dead, captured or missing. *II (Sturm)/JG4* could muster fewer than 10 out of its 25 FW190A-8s that evening. *JG6* also failed to find its allotted target of Volkel airfield; its pathfinder led the formation too far west so most attacked Heesch, home of 126 (Canadian) Wing's five Spitfire squadrons 16 km (ten miles) north-west of Volkel. The occupants were all at home as *JG6* began its attack at 0914, and No. 401 Squadron scrambled as the airfield went into action. No. 411 Squadron, airborne nearby, took a hand in the dog-fight. The Spitfires scored 24 kills that day over Heesch, for the loss of just one of their own. Bodenplatte cost *JG6* a third of its strength, including the crippling loss of six commanders—the *Geschwader Kommodore*, two of the three *Gruppen Kommandeure*, and three *Staffelkapitane*. The four deadly

RAF Tempest squadrons of 122 Wing at Volkel remained undisturbed.

An expensive victory

At Asch *JG11* strafed with little effect into a ground-mist, which did not prevent some Spitfires, Mustangs and Thunderbolts from the ten assorted Allied occupying squadrons from taking off and giving battle. German fire destroyed seven Spitfires on the ground and four Mustangs in the air, and several transport planes. It cost *JG11* 40 per cent casualties including the *Geschwader* and one of the *Gruppen* commanders with over a 100 'kills'.

III/JG77 made a few runs over Deurne and destroyed a single Typhoon, damaging about a dozen others from No. 266 Squadron. It was an expensive victory, if one considers the investment represented by 11 trained fighter pilots. Scarcely better was the strike against Grimbergen, 67 FW190 'Dora 9s' of *I/JG26*, *III/JG54* and a special *Staffel* of *JG104* found only six victims, including four B17s, on the field. A quarter of the attacking formation were shot down.

One is left with the question, Why? Seen in isolation, Bodenplatte was surely madness. The greatest possible gain was not worth the smallest possible loss.

The Allied air forces outnumbered the Luftwaffe by a huge factor, were backed by an inexhaustible supply of new machines and plenty of trained aircrew. The Luftwaffe was adequately supported by the German aircraft industry, but delivery of new equipment was increasingly unreliable, fuel was desperately short, and trained pilots were dwindling at an alarming rate.

Bodenplatte was not only unacceptable because of the high risks involved, but also because there was no longer any way to exploit such success as it achieved, either on the ground or in the air. It was the Luftwaffe's swansong.

Left A Polish fighter pilot, Flt. Lt. T. Szlenkier, of 308 Squadron, standing by the wreckage of the FW190 he shot down near Ghent

Iwo Jima, a 21 sq km (8 sq mile) island of volcanic sand might have remained in obscurity but for its strategic significance in the battle for the Pacific in World War 2. Vital to the American campaign of rolling back the newly-acquired Pacific empire of the Japanese to attack the enemy homeland, the grim battle for the tiny island lasted over a month and at the end 5800 Americans and nearly 22,000 Japanese lay dead. Seizure of the island would deny the Japanese an excellent strategic base and give the Americans a bomber base only 660 nautical miles from Tokyo. Iwo Jima was also a necessary link in the air defences of the Marianas and it had to be captured, not merely isolated. There was a final consideration—the island's fall would be a severe psychological blow to the enemy.

The US Marines played a decisive part in the drive across the Pacific, particularly in the Central Pacific advance. In their first attack, against the Gilbert Islands in November 1943, the Corps suffered heavy losses in the confused and bloody assault on Tarawa. Yet they learned a lot from the assault and now, at the beginning of 1945, the marines were preparing for their toughest assignment yet—the assault on Iwo Jima. The Japanese were also aware of Iwo Jima's importance. A garrison of 23,000 men under Lieutenant General Tadamichi Kuribayashi was sent to the island with orders to hold out for as long as possible.

The Japanese took with them 120 big guns of 75 mm calibre, 300 AA guns of over 25 mm, 20,000 small guns, including machine guns, 130 8 cm and 12 cm howitzers, 20 20 cm mortars, 70 20 cm rocket-guns, 40 47 mm and 20 37 mm AT guns, and 27 tanks. The building of pillboxes began in October 1944 and five months later 360 were complete. A superb network of deep, interconnected caves, almost impervious to naval bombardment, was built.

In overall control was Admiral Raymond Spruance's Fifth Fleet with its fast carrier and battleship units supported by a mobile fleet train. Its role was to give distance cover against enemy air or naval attack and to participate in the bombardment of the island. Rear Admiral Richmond Kelly Turner was given command of the landings. The 84,000 assault troops were to come from 4th and 5th Marine Divisions, with 3rd Marine Division in floating reserve.

'Howlin' Mad' Smith

Major General Groves B. Erskine's 3rd Division had fought at Guam and Bougainville and the 4th Division, under Major General Clifton B. Cates, had seen action at Roi-Namur, Saipan and Tinian. Major General Keller E. Rockey's 5th Division did not have combat experience but they were well trained and strengthened by many

The assault waves of Marine battalions at the moment they reached the beach of Iwo Jima. They had had a 30-minute 3658 m (4000 yd) ride to the shore. Ten destoyers, 50 gunboats, rocket craft and mortar vessels all gave close support fire, but it was all in vain. The assault would be long and bloody

veterans. Lieutenant General 'Howlin' Mad' Smith, the vigorous leader of the 1st Marine Division at Guadalcanal and now commander of the Fleet Marine Force, Pacific, was placed in an intermediate position between Spruance and Major General Harry Schmidt.

The softening-up bombing and shelling proved completely inadequate. Iwo Jima was so small that it was virtually all beach: unless enemy fire could be neutralized before the assault the Marines would be completely exposed.

With a broad rocky plateau in the north and the extinct volcano of Mount Suribachi at the southern tip of the pork-chop-shaped island, the only place a full-scale invasion could be mounted was on the black cinder beaches along the south-east coast. From this point it was only a short distance to airfield No. 1; but a landing here also meant that the open beaches would be subjected to an intense fire from higher ground to the north and the south.

At 0640 on 19 February, just before sunrise, Blandy's ships, now reinforced by two battleships and 13 cruisers from Spruance's fleet, opened up with a stupendous close-range bombardment of the island. No fewer than 450 ships ringed the island. Blasted by shells ranging from 5 in to 16 in, the beaches seemed to be torn apart. Shortly afterwards, rocket-firing gunboats attacked the Motoyama plateau while other gunboats lobbed mortar rounds at Mount Suribachi. Then, as the firing was temporarily checked and the various ships moved into their final positions, carrier aircraft and heavy bombers from the Marianas showered the areas surrounding the beaches with rockets, napalm and bombs. After a further ten minutes the naval shelling recommenced, joined by ten destroyers and over 50 gunboats which steamed as close inshore as possible in an effort to screen the steadily approaching invasion armada.

As the naval bombardment reached its crescendo, the landing-ships lowered their ramps and the first of the five assault waves emerged, 5000 m (5500 yd) from the shore. Each wave consisted of 69 armoured amphibian tractors which could take 20 troops each right onto the beach and scramble over coral reefs if necessary. The first wave, the 4th Marine Division on the right, the 5th on the left, moved towards the shore. At 0902 they hit the beach.

There were immediately two unexpected obstacles—black volcanic ash into which men sank up to a foot or more, and a steep terrace 4 m (15 ft) high in some places, which only a few tractors managed to climb. Most stayed on the beach, impeding oncoming waves, while the troops struggled through the ash. Fresh waves of assault troops arrived every five minutes and soon 10,000 men and 400 vehicles were on the beach. Despite inevitable confusion the first combat patrols pushed 130 m (150 yd) inland, then 270 (300). And then the enemy opened fire.

From rabbit-holes, bunkers and pill-boxes, small arms and machine-gun fire crashed into the Marines. Heavy artillery and mortars, from deep emplacements and caves on Suribachi and the Motoyama plateau, and trained exactly on the beaches well in advance, thundered out, destroying men and machines. The Japanese garrison, true to their orders, had withheld fire during the landings. As the momentum of the assault slowed at the terrace and the creeping barrage outdistanced the Marines, the defenders nearest the beach were able to recover and man their weapons. The ash on the beach cushioned all but direct blasts from the mortars and artillery. To stay on the beach was near-suicide—to move off it meant moving into fire from the defence system.

Marines of 5th Division pinned down in the volcanic ash of the beach they had landed on. Four days would pass before Mount Suribachi, in the background, was taken. After that, two long months of mopping up followed

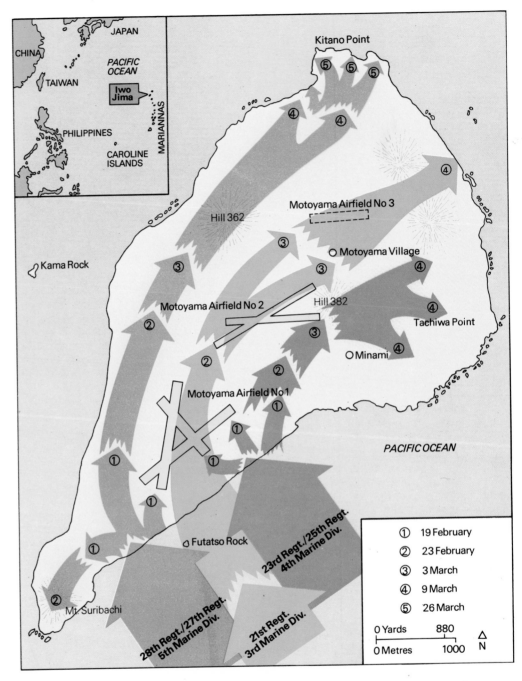

The five bitter phases of the protracted struggle to capture Iwo Jima's 21 sq km (8 sq miles). Some 30,000 Marines were put ashore on the first day, and ten days later there were 84,000 Marines fighting the prepared-to-die Japanese

①	19 February
②	23 February
③	3 March
④	9 March
⑤	26 March

0 Yards 880
0 Metres 1000

At this point the outcome of the battle was in doubt. If the Japanese had mounted a counterattack, they might have routed the disorganized Marines. But the Japanese had orders to deny Iwo Jima to the enemy for as long as possible and their troops were ordered to stay strictly on the defensive. The initiative still lay with the Marines—they and their equipment were successfully ashore. Now they must go forward.

Desperately slowly, the Marines pushed inland, a confused collection of small groups rather than a united force. Each bunker, each rabbit-hole meant a fight to the death. Each enemy position was sup-ported by many others—the Japanese would disappear down one hole and pop up at another, often behind rather than in front of the advancing Marines. The Marines struggled on, pouring bullets, grenades and flame into enemy positions. Flail tanks rumbled forward with the Marines, detonating land mines, tank-dozers carved channels through the terrace and ordinary tanks relieved the pressure on the Marines by knocking out machine-gun nests and pillboxes. But it was no pushover. Facing 4th Division's lines were ten reinforced concrete blockhouses, seven covered artillery positions and 80 pillboxes. Whenever a man showed himself it was almost certain death. By mid-afternoon the reserve battalions, four regimental combat teams and two tank battalions, had been committed to relieve the pressure on the leading units.

As dusk fell on this first, bloody day, the number of Marines had risen to 30,000. On the left flank Colonel Harry B. Liversedge's 28th Regiment had pushed across to the ridge which overlooked the beaches on the south-west; but fierce enemy opposition had halted its progress towards its main target, Mount Suribachi. Next in line was Colonel Thomas A. Wornham's 27th Regiment, which had similarly been brought to a halt in its efforts to overrun airfield No. 1. Farther to the right were the two regiments of the 4th Division, Colonel Walter W. Wensinger's 23rd Marines and Colonel John R. Lanigan's 25th Marines; both had come under extremely heavy fire from the entire Motoyama plateau area, and the 25th Regiment, being farthest on the right, suffered many casualties—one battalion had only 150 men left in the front line.

Although the Marines had failed to reach their first day's objectives, they had secured a foothold and were digging in to await the expected counter-attack. It didn't come. Instead, the Japanese sent deadly accurate mortar and artillery fire against

the beaches, causing great loss of life. Most feared were the 60 and 250 kg bombs which the Japanese had converted into rockets, which burst upon impact.

On the second morning, after a 50-minute naval bombardment, the Marines moved on again. But progress was even slower. Liversedge's 28th Regiment, making repeated attacks upon the approaches to Mount Suribachi, advanced only 180 m (200 yd) that day. To the north the 4th Division reached their objectives on No. 1 airfield and then swung right to face the rising ground of Kuribayashi's first major defence line. Early progress soon petered out. On the next day this line remained virtually static but the 28th Regiment, assisted by naval and aerial bombardment, penetrated almost to the foot of Suribachi.

Mountain symbol of mastery

Rising steeply out of the sea to a height of 170 m (556 ft) the mountain was not of central importance to the defence of Iwo Jima. Yet it offered fine observation and artillery siting positions and control of it tended to symbolize mastery of the island. Recognizing that it would soon be cut off, Kuribayashi had allocated only 1860 men to its defence; several hundred blockhouses, pillboxes and covered guns had been built

US Coast Guards assist a wounded Marine, hit when his amtrac took a direct mortar hit. Coast Guard-manned landing craft swiftly evacuated casualties to hospital ships, where the medical treatment was the best of the Pacific war

Marines crouch behind a rock
and take cover as a satchel-
carried explosive charge
destroys a cave entrance to
Japanese defences. There
were 365 pillboxes, 46
blockhouses and some 90
artillery emplacements to be
taken this way

were left and every one was to be fought for.

Kuribayashi had turned the plateau
region into an armed camp. Rockets,
artillery and mortars, one a 320 mm weapon
that lobbed 315 kg (700 lb) shells, were
plentiful and blockhouses and pillboxes
were numerous. Caves were elaborate and
well-fortified—one could hold 2000 troops
and had 12 exits—and the defenders were
well-trained and in high morale. They were
prepared to hold a position to the death,
infiltrate Marine lines, or throw themselves
under an enemy tank with a bomb strapped
to their backs. It was all deadly, fright-
eningly inhuman.

But this was exactly what the Marines
were trained for. During the Pacific War the
Marines endured a much more savage, personal and individual form of combat than
that seen in the actions in Western Europe
or North Africa, and against a fanatical
enemy who would not surrender. There
was no room for manoeuvre, or indirect
approach, on this battlefield—it was one of
total assault.

The Japanese positions were bombarded
by warships, ranging from destroyers'
5 in guns to battleships' 16 in guns,
they were battered by heavy bombers,
strafed by rockets and machine-guns of
fighters, assaulted by dive-bombers.
Tanks, artillery, mortar and rocket firers
hammered the positions, flame-throwers
scorched them, dynamite blasted them.
But the Marines knew that the capture
of virtually every position also involved
brutal close-in fighting—with machine-gun,
pistol, grenade, knife, digging-tool, even
hands—before the defenders were fully
overcome.

The battle for the second airfield, in the
centre of the island, was typical. Hundreds
of pillboxes, rabbit-holes and concealed
emplacements defied the concentrated
American fire-power for two days. On 24
February, the two battalions of the 21st
Marine Regiment rushed foward to take the
enemy lines with bayonet and grenade. Not
only did the Japanese fire upon them, but
many rushed into the open and engaged
in hand-to-hand combat. Casualties rose
steeply on both sides. The Marines, thrown
back, re-formed and charged again. By
nightfall of the next day, they had captured
the airfield and were pressing towards
Motoyama village, with the prospect of
another bitter struggle ahead: to the right of
them lay the formidable Hill 382.

Nothing but a heap of stones
By the tenth day of the fighting, though,
the supporting fire for the 3rd Division had
been substantially increased, the forward

around its base together with an intricate
system of caves in the slopes. As always,
each position had to be taken separately,
using mortars, tanks, rockets, flame-
throwers and dynamite. When the Marines
reached the caves, they went in with knives
to kill the Japanese in close combat. Some of
the defenders, out of ammunition, were
reduced to rolling stones down the slopes,
but still they fought on. By the morning of 23
February, the Marines were approaching
the summit and 40 men under Lieutenant
Harold Schrier carried an American flag to
signify their victory. At 1020 it was raised
amid cheers while fighting was still going on
in the vicinity; and at noon it was replaced
by a much larger flag. The photograph
taken became probably the most famous of
the entire war.

The end was far from in sight—the worst
had yet to come. Anticipating a fierce
struggle, the Americans had committed the
3rd Marine Division on the same day to
the middle of the front line, with the 4th
on the right and the 5th on the left, and
General Schmidt had come ashore to take
direct control of what was the largest group
of Marines yet to fight under a single
command. Only 2400 m (2630 yd) of island

battalions found a weak spot in the Japanese line and poured through. By evening Moto-yama, now a heap of stones and rubble, was taken and the Marines could look down upon the third airfield. Once again, further momentum was broken by Kuribayashi's second major defence line, and there remained many areas to wipe up. Hill 382 was fiercely held by its defenders for two more days, and Hill 362 in the west was equally difficult. The whole operation was taking much longer than the ten days Schmidt had estimated for it. Some units were down to 30 per cent of their original strength. On Sunday 5 March, the three divisions regrouped and rested as best they could in the face of Japanese shelling and occasional infiltration.

For the Japanese, the situation was critical. Most of Kuribayashi's tanks and guns and over two-thirds of his officers had been lost. His troops were in a serious position, reduced to such desperate measures as strapping explosives to their backs and throwing themselves under American tanks. The Marines were moving relentlessly forward, however slowly, and this forced a gradual breakdown in Kuri-bayashi's communications system. This meant that, left to their own devices, individual Japanese officers tended to revert to the offensive. One attack, by 1000 naval troops on the night of 8-9 March, was easily repulsed by 4th Marine Division with Japanese losses of over 800 men.

On the afternoon of 9 March, a patrol from the 3rd Marine Division reached the north-eastern coast of Iwo Jima. There was no stopping the Americans but even now there was no sign of Japanese surrender.

On 14 March the Americans, believing all organized resistance to be at an end, declared Iwo Jima occupied and raised the Stars and Stripes. But in their warren of caves and tunnels, the Japanese lived on. Clearing out pockets of organized resist-ance with tanks, demolition teams, rifle fire and flamethrowers took until 26 March. On this day the Japanese staged their last desperate fling when 350 troops rushed an Air Force and Seabee construction camp. They were destroyed by a Marine pioneer battalion after a day of wild fighting. Kuribayashi committed suicide in the northern corner of Iwo Jima in the last few days of the battle.

Only 216 Japanese had surrendered by 26 March; 20,000 were dead. In the following two months 1600 Japanese were killed and another 370 captured as sporadic resist-ance was crushed. The American casualties were equally daunting. A total of 275 officers and 5610 men of the Marine Corps were killed and 826 officers and 16,446 men were wounded. Thirty per cent of the entire landing force and a staggering 75 per cent of the infantry regiments of the 4th and 5th Divisions were battle casualties. Twenty-four Medals of Honour were awarded and there were 2648 'combat fatigue casu-alties'—both facts telling evidence of the gruelling nature of the battle for Iwo Jima.

Iwo Jima soon justified the strategic value which the Joint Chiefs of Staff and, in particular, the Air Force had attached to it. Before the end of the war against Japan, more than 20,000 crewmen in crippled planes had landed upon the island's airstrips; and from 7 April onwards, thanks to the efforts of the Seabee construction units, Mustang fighters were able to escort the daylight raids of the Superfortresses against Tokyo and other Japanese cities.

The photograph that came to symbolize Iwo Jima and the struggle to clear the Japanese from the Pacific island chains. The Stars and Stripes is dug into the lava rim of Mount Suribachi, flying from a Japanese iron pipe

THE RHINE CROSSINGS

A young Commando lay with his comrades, blackened face pressed to the dank Rhineland soil, waiting and listening.

The RAF dropped 1100 tons of HE on Wesel, just north of the Ruhr, on 23-24 March. The bomb bays of the 200 Lancasters of No. 3 Group RAF had been equipped to hold a great variety of HE bombs, from 1360 kg (4000 lb) 'Cookies' to 9980 kg (22,000 lb) Grand Slams. As the last of them turned for base the men of 1st Commando Brigade, shaken, dazed and slightly deaf, made their way towards the ruins of the town glowing red through the swirling smoke, sparks and dust. Within minutes the familiar chatter of a Spandau was heard, soon to be joined by others. Tracer streaked towards the attackers.

The Commandos had trained on the Maas for the Rhine crossing and went about their business with the assurance of experts. Artillery preparation had commenced at 1700 and at 2100 about 3500 guns opened up a violent barrage to cover the Scottish battalions forming the first wave of the attack. According to the Allied Supreme Commander in Europe, General Dwight D. Eisenhower, it was the 'largest and most difficult amphibious operation undertaken since the landings in Normandy'.

In March three powerful Allied army groups closed up to the Rhine. General Jacob L. Dever's 6th, with the US Seventh and the French First Army under command, formed Eisenhower's right wing, the French facing the Siegfried Line covering the Black Forest, the Americans on their left flank opposite Karlsruhe. In the centre stood General Omar N. Bradley's 12th Army Group, with the US First and Third Armies holding a wide front from south of Dusseldorf to Mannheim. On 7 March General Courtney H. Hodges' First Army had seized the Ludendorff Bridge at Remagen intact, and was steadily consolidating this lodgement. On the left flank was 21st Army Group with, from left to right, the Canadian First, British Second and US Ninth Armies under command. Eisenhower intended that the 12th and 6th Army Groups should also assault the Rhine barrier as opportunity arose.

It was clear that the last great Allied offensive in the West was about to begin. For senior professional soldiers it offered a last chance of glory, a final opportunity to set a seal on their careers. To the Americans, who had by far the greatest number of troops in the field, it appeared that Montgomery was trying to steal the limelight as he went methodically about the preparations for mounting Operation

Troops of the 89th Division, US Third Army, keep their heads down as they cross the Rhine at Oberwesel in an amphibious craft. Once the Rhine was crossed the conquest of Germany followed swiftly

Left A heavy tank, an M26, is rolled on to a pontoon by soldiers of a pontoon battalion, near Remagen

'Plunder', the code-name for the Rhine crossings.

The British would assault with two Corps and the Ninth Army with one. A Canadian brigade would take part in the British attack. That Bradley should belittle the meticulous approach of Montgomery is no suprise. Hodges was not concerned with criticizing the performance of others so much as re-establishing his reputation. The seizing of the Remagen bridge had gone a long way towards that. Though the terrain beyond the bridge did not lend itself to immediate and significant exploitation, there was no question that the thrust had touched the enemy at a vital spot. Hodges meant to take every advantage of it. General George S. Patton, the commander of US Third Army, was no admirer of Montgomery's deliberate methods. A friend of Bradley's, he was obsessed with the idea of beating the Field-Marshal across the Rhine.

On the far right flank, General Jean de Lattre de Tassigny, at the head of the French First Army, was equally determined to get into the act. Montgomery had something to prove. He had long argued the cause of the single thrust into the heart of Nazi Germany. It was his intention to establish a great armoured force across the river and there was no reason why this tank avalanche should not crash through to Berlin 400 km (250 miles) east. Brussels, 320 km (200 miles) from the Normandy beachhead, had fallen swiftly once the break-out was achieved.

There was something in the Rhine crossing for everyone—except the Germans. The burden weighed particularly heavily on the shoulders of 60-year-old Field-Marshal Albert Kesselring. Renowned for his stubborn and skilful defence of the Italian peninsula, Kesselring was called to Berlin on 8 March 1945 and briefed by Hitler to hold the line of the Rhine and win time for the introduction of the wonder weapons

expected to avert catastrophe. Even as outlined by the deluded Hitler the prospects for Germany were bleak that chill spring. The Russians stood within practical striking distance of Berlin. Allied aircraft dominated German skies.

Kesselring was ordered to eliminate the Remagen bridgehead and to secure the great barrier while a decision was reached in the East. He received his field marshal's baton as a Luftwaffe commander and drove to his new HQ at Ziegenburg, near Frankfurt, constructed as a Fuehrer command post for the Blitzkrieg of 1940. But a miracle was required. The only thing he could be sure would hold its position in the impending battle was the Rhine itself.

Model's men in a state of exhaustion

On paper at least, Kesselring deployed formations similar to Eisenhower's forces along the Rhine. In Holland and along the Lower Rhine 67-year-old Colonel General Johannes Blaskowitz's Army Group H was stationed. He could deploy about 85,000 men to hold off Montgomery, including the crack First Parachute Army which had fought so fiercely during the Rhineland struggle west of the river. Few of its men had made a parachute jump but their training and fanaticism made them formidable opponents. And from 10 March any of Blaskowitz's soldiers away from his unit was liable to be summarily tried and shot. In the centre Field Marshal Walther Model commanded Army Group B with responsibility for the Ruhr. His force totalled around 350,000 men. Their quality varied. After successive defeats many officers and men had been reduced to a dangerous state of exhaustion. Some were nervous wrecks and there was a grave shortage of junior officers. On the left flank commanding Army Group G was 65-year-old Colonel General Paul Hausser, an ex-Wehrmacht regular who had joined the Waffen SS.

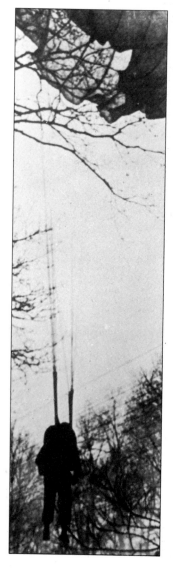

Below A dead American paratrooper shot by a German sniper after becoming entangled in the branches of a tree. It was a common hazard and often led to the same fate since the man is comparatively helpless in this position

This map shows the Allied bridgeheads established along the length of the Rhine. Despite Hitler's insistence that the Rhine must be held, the German army was weapon-starved and no match for the vast, well-armed Allied armies, massed to thrust deep into the heart of the Third Reich

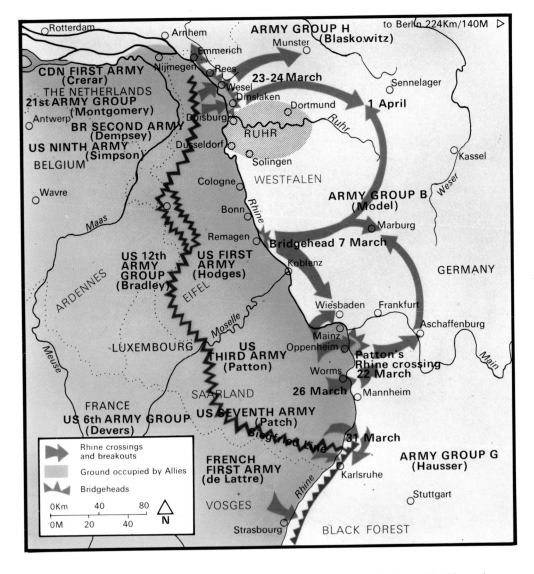

There were more than 60 German divisions along the whole front, but these varied enormously in quality. The 25 new *Volksgrenadier* divisions, formed after July 1944, had a paper establishment of 10,000 men but many had been filled with untrained reinforcements. Many of the heavy weapons had been transferred to the Oder and Kesselring was forced to rely on the 88 mm AA/AT gun as the backbone of his defence. As the Allied air forces had switched to the battle zones, the redeployment of the Luftwaffe's flak Corps in the forward areas was a logical move. Simple field works were dug covering likely crossing places along the river and large numbers of mines were sown along the banks.

The area of 21st Army Group west of the river had been the scene of bitter fighting until 10 March. It was into this zone that the Allied lines of communication had to be extended. Bridges of all shapes and sizes

had to be built and about 50,000 engineers and pioneers were eventually employed. To conceal this a massive daytime smoke screen was maintained from 16 March by the Royal Pioneer Corps. More than 250,000 tons of stores were dumped, mainly by night, and 36 Royal Navy landing craft were brought overland from Antwerp to Nijmegen ready for use on the Rhine.

The area selected for the assault was a 50 km (30 mile) stretch of the Rhine between Emmerich in the north and the edge of the Ruhr near Dinslaken in the south. Three Corps were to attack—from left to right the British 30th and 12th Corps, and the US 16th Corps. The river was about 550 m (500 yd) wide, a plain dotted with abandoned farms running down to the water on the westward side. The eastern shore climbed gradually to higher wooded ground. February floods had left areas under water to add to the problems of the attackers on the far side. It was expected that these difficulties would be overcome by the use of specialized armour and amphibious support vehicles which had been assembled.

A heavy responsibility was placed on the British 79th Armoured Division. The brainchild of Major-General Sir Percy C. S. Hobart, who commanded it, the Division had formed the cutting edge of the British in the D-Day landings of June 1944. By the spring of 1945 it was one of the most powerful assault forces in the world, a score of regiments containing armoured vehicles to meet any situation.

'Funnies' come into their own

As on D-Day, tanks would land in close support of the infantry and extra units, including elements of a US battalion, were trained to use Duplex Drive (DD) Shermans. With canvas screens erected these tanks were powered across waterways by a small propeller and went into action immediately they grounded. To ease their path, an Armoured Vehicle Royal Engineer laid an improvised 'carpet' over bad going. As deep mud was a problem on the Rhine and would slow the DD tanks, the 'bobbins' carrying the carpets were mounted on yet another of 79th Division's 'Funnies'— a tracked landing vehicle known as the Buffalo.

This had been tested in action in Belgium and Holland during the autumn. Propelled by specially-designed tracks, it mounted a light cannon and two machine-guns and could carry either troops, a field gun, a Bren carrier, a bulldozer or two tons of cargo. Because the soft going was expected to hamper the DD tanks, the Buffaloes were earmarked to spearhead the Rhine attack.

There were 600 of them in 21st Army Group and most of them would be used to land assault infantry. Once sufficient armour was established the Buffaloes would bring over more infantry while rafts were used to ferry over heavy equipment.

Montgomery intended to attack with elements of six divisions at staggered times on the night of 23-24 March and to follow up with an airborne landing on the 24th. A few hours before, news arrived from the South. Patton had sent six battalions across the Rhine at Oppenheim where the river was only half the width of the Lower Rhine. The crossing met weak opposition and there were few casualties. Strategically its potential was restricted. The penetration was made south of a tributary of the Rhine, the Main, which lay on its flanks and would have to be crossed in its turn. Nevertheless on 23 March Patton had a bridgehead 10 km (6 miles) deep and wide. His tanks were crossing on 'treadway' bridges. German resistance was only token—at least in the battle area.

The Oppenheim crossing created a sensation in Berlin. The Rhine was virtually unguarded at this point. Not satisfied with his exploit, Patton tried other attacks across the Rhine gorge where the cliffs rose 120 m (400 ft). But his troops ran into trouble and were pulled back.

The pressure on the German High Command had by now become intense. Widespread bombing and fighter-bomber attacks had disrupted communications even more than usual. The forces containing the Remagen bridgehead were consuming all reinforcements sent to them, and there were signs of another great blow coming on

Men of the US-equipped French First Army board barges to cross the Rhine. General de Gaulle had pressed the importance to French morale of their presence in the crossings. They were led by the brilliant General de Lattre de Tassigny

The points along the Rhine where General Montgomery's armies forced their crossings and established the subsequent bridgehead for a drive into the heart of Germany

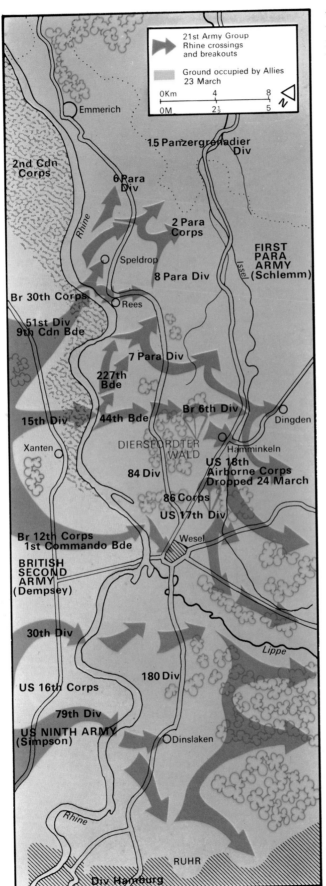

Map legend:
21st Army Group Rhine crossings and breakouts

Ground occupied by Allies 23 March

0Km 4 8
0M 2½ 5

the Lower Rhine. It fell at 2100 on 23 March when the great barrage opened up and Buffaloes nosed into the Rhine and deposited the 7th Black Watch on the eastern shore near Rees. The 7th Argyll and Sutherland Highlanders landed soon afterwards.

Meanwhile, the Commandos crossed in Buffaloes to establish a bridgehead, others in storm-boats. North of Wesel, the 15th Scottish Division opened the 12th Corps attack at 0200, landing unscathed near Xanten. The leading battalions of the right brigade, the 44th, met little resistance as they advanced. But, on the left, the 227th Brigade ran into nests of Spandaus dug into the sides of flood dykes and manned by 7th Parachute Division. The 10th Highland Light Infantry and 2nd Argylls engaged in close combat and the 2nd Gordon Highlanders came up in support but the enemy resisted stoutly.

The enemy's nerve is broken

At the same time, US Ninth Army launched its 30th Division south of Wesel, but the enemy's nerve was broken by the hour-long barrage in which 65,000 shells were fired and 1500 bombers plastered rear areas. An hour later, at 0300, 79th Division landed two regiments. The price of Ninth Army's foothold across the Rhine was 31 killed and wounded.

As the light improved both Scottish divisions met areas of strong opposition with counter-attacks by infantry and self-propelled guns (SPGs). Some Highlanders had been cut off in Speldrop but were holding out. Enemy mortars were active and a salvo of bombs cost 51st Division its commander, Major-General Thomas G. Renie, killed as he returned from visiting forward locations. The delay in capturing Rees held up bridging operations but rafts were ferrying heavy loads, including tanks and armoured personnel carriers. In the US sector a bridge would soon be built.

Shortly before 1000 on the 24th the Allied guns fell silent and a vast air fleet thundered into sight. The US 18th Airborne Corps had arrived. Of its two divisions, the US 17th had set off from 12 airfields near Paris and the British flew from England. They met over Wavre, Belgium. It took more than two and a half hours for the 1572 aircraft and 1300 gliders to pass a given point. Commanded by US Major General Matthew B. Ridgeway, who had British Major-General Richard N. Gale, DSO, as his deputy, the airborne forces were ordered to 'disrupt the hostile defence of the Rhine in the Wesel sector by the seizure of key terrain'.

The main objectives were behind the Diersfordter Wald where the airborne troops were to seize the cross roads at Hamminkeln and bridges across the River Issel. Code-name for this operation was 'Varsity'. Applying techniques developed after Arnhem, the 16,870 attackers landed in tactical groups close to their targets, covered by their own guns and 12th Corps' 540 pieces.

The parachute element landed first and was met with fierce fire from light AA and machine-guns. The US aircraft carrying British brigades were caught as they flew out and suffered heavily. Of the 242 planes which carried the paratroops of 6th Airborne Division, 18 were shot down and 115 damaged.

Heavier fire was opened up on the gliders and tugs which followed the parachute drop. The smoke from burning buildings in Wesel and from crashed aircraft shrouded the landing zones and many pilots were forced to crash their gliders where they could. More than half the British 6th Air Landing Brigade gliders were hit and the Americans suffered similar casualties. Gliders often burst into flames on landing and the troops ran into fire as they scrambled out. Armoured cars and SPGs shot up the area causing many casualties. The deadly 88s were also ready when 240 Liberators of 8th USAAF roared in to drop 600 tons of follow-up supplies and equipment; 16 four-engined giants were added to the blazing wreckage.

Out of this apparent chaos a hopeful picture gradually emerged. Though the river crossings were costly, they enabled troops to seize their objectives. Tanks and SPGs attempted counter-attacks but were repulsed. From 1030 when the gliders came down, to mid-afternoon, both sides fought furiously at close range. The 1st Royal

Ulster Rifles suffered most of the casualties they recorded that day—16 officers and 243 other ranks. The 12th Devonshire Regiment and 2nd Oxfordshire and Buckinghamshire Light Infantry, the other units in 6th Air Landing Brigade, also suffered heavily. But by 1100 Hamminkeln and a number of bridges had been captured. In the afternoon 15th Scottish Division established contact with both airborne divisions. The Commandos were also in touch with the Americans. Ninth Army had also made vital progress and had thrown a bridge across the Rhine by 1620 on the 24th.

The Germans counter-attacked during the night, and more street fighting took place. The situation remained serious around Speldrop where the entire 9th

Above Desperate German infantry armed with Panzerfaust fight a last-ditch action against the unstoppable advancing Allied soldiers

Left Hitler's policy of no retreat exacted a fearful toll in German lives. British infantry make their way past enemy dead, already searched for intelligence-useful material

Above US infantry advance past a knocked-out French Chaffe M24 light tank on the outskirts of Rhineburg, just a mile from the river

Below German civilians began to surrender too. These people are now homeless and hungry; Hitler's promises had come to nothing

Canadian Brigade (3rd Division) was drawn into 51st Division's battle. It was two days before the Highland Light Infantry of Canada and the North Nova Scotia Highlanders secured Speldrop and enabled the Black Watch to withdraw.

More bridges, more ferries brought over Montgomery's armoured divisions. Long before the last defiant defenders were overcome, fresh infantry divisions were streaming into the bridgehead, which, by the evening of the 27th was 55 km (35 miles) wide and 30 km (20 miles) deep with 16,259 prisoners for the price of 6781 casualties.

On 25 March, in Eisenhower's centre, three corps of the US first Army burst out of the Remagen bridgehead and swung round the southern face of the Ruhr. A strong armoured force drove south the following day to link up with Patton's troups near Wiesbaden. Patton himself was attacking across the Main at Aschaffenburg.

The German line begins to crumble

On the right wing, Devers had sent Lieutenant General Alexander M. Patch's Seventh Army across the Rhine at Worms early on 26th March and by the evening the American penetration was 11 km (seven miles) deep. Swinging north the Seventh Army contacted Patton's Third. The German line was beginning to crumble. Patch's push north inevitably stretched the front of the 6th Army Group and led to the French First Army extending its left. De Lattre immediately ordered preparations for an assault crossing. On 29 March he was told by General Charles de Gaulle: 'You must cross the Rhine. It is a matter of the greatest national interest.'

Devers asked on 30 March when the French might be ready to cross and was mildly surprised to learn they would attack the following morning. The 3rd Algerian Division got over in the early hours of 31 March and with one rubber dinghy ferrying ten men at a time established an assault company before the Germans became aware of their presence. Nearer Karlsruhe, 2nd Moroccan Division ran into trouble because its hastily mounted attack was delayed until daybreak.

Only 30 men reached the shore from the first wave of 200 and hung on until reinforcements arrived. While the build-up went on the French artillery fired furiously and broke up all attempts to drive back the invaders. On 1-2 April de Lattre made a third crossing and used American bridges to reinforce his troops on Karlsruhe. The Rhine was no longer a barrier.

For the German Army the most ominous sign was the breakdown of communications. Kesselring could not contact Model who remained in the Ruhr fortress, where more than 300,000 men had less than three weeks' rations. The US First and Ninth Armies sealed the ring around Army Group B on 1 April.

All the Allied generals who took part in the Rhine crossings had success. Montgomery in particular had realized his intentions by placing a force of 20 divisions with 1500 tanks at the gates to the Westphalian plain. His reward was to lose control of Ninth US Army and to see the major offensive role transferred to Bradley. Also destroyed was his dream of the Allies taking Berlin. Eisenhower was now bent solely on eliminating the last remnants of Hitler's forces.

The crossing of the Rhine was a famous victory. Whether Eisenhower and his advisers realized the significance of it is another matter. The way to Berlin and final victory was open.

On 22 September 1944 Eisenhower told his senior commanders: 'The envelopment of the Ruhr from the north by 21st Army Group supported by First US Army is the main effort of the present phase of operations.' A great airborne operation, 'Market Garden', was to turn the German right flank and put Montgomery's 21st Army Group on the Lower Rhine north of the Ruhr.

Montgomery's right wing, Ninth US Army, drove forward 80 km (50 miles) and by 5 March held the west bank of the Rhine from Moers to Dusseldorf; by 6 March the left of General Omar N. Bradley's 12th Army Group, First US Army, had advanced to Euskirchen and Cologne. On 7 March its tanks boldly seized the Ludendorff railway bridge at Remagen and Bradley unhesitatingly pushed four divisions across the Rhine. The rapid build-up of this 25 km (15 mile) bridgehead along the Rhine's east bank transformed Allied strategy. Until the opportunity to exploit from Remagen, Eisenhower had apparently decided the long, acrimonious debate about a single thrust or broad front advance into Germany in Montgomery's favour. He told the Joint Chiefs of Staff in early February 1945 that he would cross the Rhine with maximum strength in the north without waiting to close the river barrier throughout its length. But the rapid expansion of the Remagen bridgehead and Lieutenant General George S. Patton's Third US Army's sudden Rhine crossing at Oppenheim on 22 March, made him reconsider.

Although Hitler's battle maps showed 60 German divisions in the West, these were the true equivalent of 23 infantry divisions and six Panzer divisions, in reality each not much stronger than a *Kampfgruppe*, about one-third of a division. They faced attacks from 94 full-strength Allied divisions, of which 22 were armoured. Against the 10,000 aircraft of the Allied air forces the Luftwaffe could put up barely 1000 of which only 80 were the new jet-fighters. Even allowing for the superiority of German tanks, AT guns, *Panzerfausts*, jet fighters, and her soldiers' skills, it was plain that the uneven struggle would not be protracted.

Field Marshal Walther Model, commander of Army Group B centered in the Ruhr, had no illusions about the battle's outcome but decided that a determined defence of the Ruhr was not merely his duty but would delay the invasion of Germany.

By late March 1945 the converging attacks of Montgomery's Ninth US Army and Bradley's First US Army had squeezed three German armies along the Middle Rhine front between the rivers Lippe and Sieg, Army Group B's sector.

These three armies totalled 19 depleted divisions minus much heavy equipment lost in attempting to escape across the Rhine. In Army Group B there were only 65 tanks, of which 50 were fighting along the northern

The Third Reich now knew the real meaning of invasion. A 76 mm-gun Sherman tank of 35th US Infantry Division's 748th Tank Battalion passes through the shattered city of Gelsenkirchen, north-east of Essen, on 10 April 1945

Above Maj. Gen. Maurice Rose, of 3rd Armored Division (right) at a unit citation ceremony. He was killed in action a week later

crossings over the river Dill, 30 km (20 miles) south of Siegen.

By nightfall on the fourth day, 28 March, 3rd Armored's Combat Command B had reached Marburg, 130 km (80 miles) from the start-line. Combat Command R was at Killenberg and Combat Command A held Herborn, 40 km (25 miles) farther back. Model's left flank had been decisively turned. Ninth US Army's 2nd Armored Division, on Montgomery's extreme right, pushed the southern boundary of their Wesel bridgehead through the Lippe river valley as far as Dorsten, effectively turning Model's right flank as well.

periphery of the Remagen bridgehead. The whole of the Ruhr was combed for weapons, those not actively engaged in the fighting were left nothing but pistols. For the coming Allied onslaught Model would deploy about a quarter of a million men, some untrained, some tough veterans.

Anticipated frontal assault

Fifth Panzer Army's staff anticipated a frontal assault across the Rhine between Duisburg and Dusseldorf combined with a renewed thrust across the Sieg river, in a pincer movement to cut off the south-west quarter of the Ruhr. Model moved his battle HQ to Olpe, a road and rail center 55 km (35 miles) east of Cologne and 20 km (12 miles) north of the Sieg.

The main attack south of the Ruhr was to be made by Major General 'Lightning Joe' Lawton Collins' 7th Corps of First US Army; its 78th Infantry Division was to hold the Sieg river line while 1st Infantry Division protected the Corps' north flank and 3rd Armored Division was given the task of deep penetration. On 25 March 1945 3rd Armored's three combat commands, each strengthened by a battalion of infantry, broke out of the Remagen bridgehead heading for Altenkirchen 25 km (15 miles) ahead through hilly wooded country. Once there the division would drive east to secure

Below Field Marshal Model, the trusted 'fireman' of Adolf Hitler

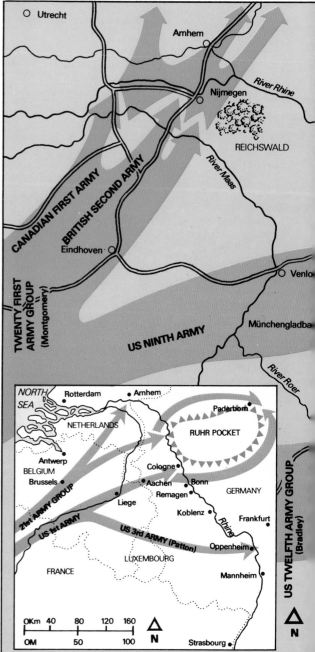

The Allied advances north and south of the Ruhr were part of a general north-east movement of the front from Arnhem to Strasbourg which threatened to leave a third of a million German soldiers in an ever-deepening Ruhr pocket. Army Group B's commander was aware of his danger.

Colonel General Johannes von Blasko-witz's Army Group H in the north was being driven back, its south wing threatened by the deteriorating position of Model's Army Group B. The two commanders asked permission to withdraw behind the Weser river and there form a strong new front. Hitler ordered all forces to stand and fight, decreeing the death penalty for any commanders abandoning any inhabited place. These orders condemned Army Group B to certain defeat.

American success in the Ruhr encouraged Eisenhower to announce his decision: Bradley would be given the main role in the final offensive while Montgomery protected Bradley's left flank and cleared northern Germany to the Danish frontier. After the Ruhr was encircled, Ninth US Army would revert to Bradley's command but the drive to the Elbe would be delayed until Model's forces in the Ruhr had been safely eliminated from the war.

Within eight days of crossing the Rhine, the Allies linked up 120 km (75 miles) beyond at Lippstadt. After 18 more days they had encircled the whole of German Army Group B

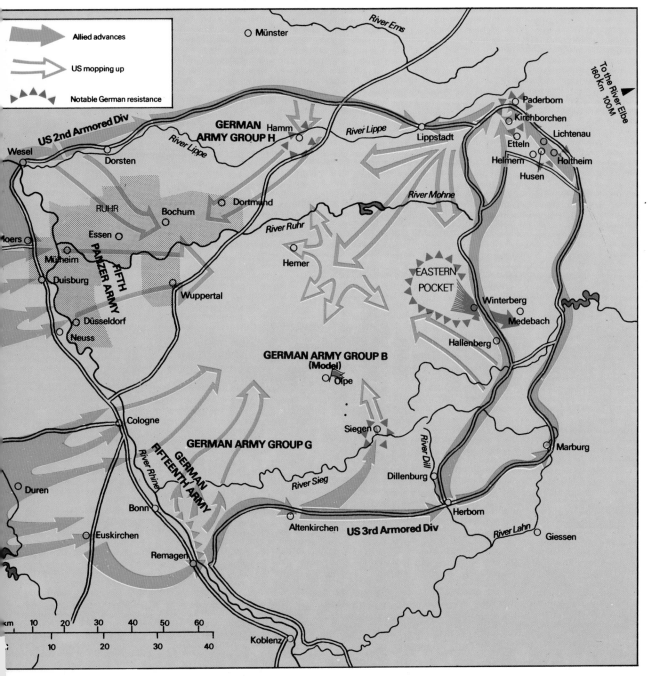

The Gateway to Germany—the famous Ludendorff railway bridge over the Rhine at Remagen. It fell intact into Allied hands on 7 March and became the spring-board for the pincer attack on the Ruhr starting 25 March

After four days' continuous advancing with very little rest the men of 3rd Armored Division's six Task Forces were feeling rather pleased with their progress. Then Major General Maurice Rose, commander of the 3rd Armored Division, was ordered to get to Paderborn and just keep on going until they reached the high ground at Paderborn airport.

On Good Friday, 30 March 1945, the leading reconnaissance forces were engaged and Task Force Richardson and Task Force Hogan quickly moved up to shatter the resistance. They were met by intense *Panzerfaust* and small-arms fire. In Kirchborchen, only 6 km (4 miles) short of Paderborn, Task force Richardson found these rockets coming at them from every angle and were lucky to lose only two Shermans. The armoured infantry suffered grievously from concentrated machine-gun and light AA fire. Despite American numerical superiority and tremendous fire-power—there were only 200 Germans and no tanks in the town—Task Force Richardson was held for 24 hours.

The other Task Forces also met stubborn German resistance. Colonel John C. Welborn's soldiers took all day to clear the little towns of Husen and Etteln, then broke clear along a minor road running east and turned north towards Paderborn. There seemed to be no resistance but four Tiger tanks ambushed the American column, knocking out seven Shermans and subjecting the rest to systematic 88 mm and machine-gun fire while six more Tigers cut in from the south-east to completely surround Task Force Welborn.

Brigadier General Doyle O. Hickey, Combat Command A commander, took over the division. All during 31 March the bitter, uneven battle for Paderborn raged; the outnumbered, weaker German force fought with extraordinary tenacity, only yielding at last to concentrated mortar fire, shelling from heavy artillery and incineration by flamethrowers. In the end, infantry of 104th Division were brought up to storm the Lichtenau/Etteln sector before 3rd Armored's tanks and guns could make their planned co-ordinated attack on Paderborn.

This was to take place on Easter Sunday 1 April but Major General Collins, 7th Corps commander, was worried about reports of German preparations for a counter-attack against his long, thinly-held line. After initial confusion, the Germans reacted violently to the American breakthrough south of the Ruhr: the 8th Infantry Division, in attempting to seize Siegen, met fierce resistance from the newly-trained 12th *Volksgrenadier* Division which flung itself against the Sieg river crossings with some of the *Wehrmacht*'s old style. Farther north in rough, mountainous country near Winterberg, 9th US Infantry Division was hit hard by a force of Panzers and infantry from Bayerlein's *Kampfgruppe*. Forced to withdraw, the Americans dug in.

In a highly unorthodox move, 'Lightning Joe' Collins telephoned his old friend, Lieutenant General William H. Simpson, Ninth US Army commander, and asked him to send a combat command from 2nd Armored Division east towards Paderborn.

At the same time he would order 3rd Armored Division to detach a Task Force to meet it. Without consulting Montgomery about this major tactical change, Simpson sent a combat command racing through the night to Lippstadt, there to link up with troops of First US Army. At 0300 on the morning of Easter Sunday, Task Force Kane of 3rd Armored Division was ordered to break off its attack on Paderborn, swing 90 degrees west and advance some 30 km (20 miles) towards Lippstadt 'to make contact with the 2nd Armored Division'.

Armoured infantry reach outskirts of town

By 0500 the leading vehicles of 2nd Armored Division were about 8 km (5 miles) from Lippstadt. At the same time the leading light tanks of Task Force Kane were moving west towards Lippstadt whose garrison commander was ordered to defend it to the last man. Hastily improvised tank traps were thrown across every road and every man and boy able to bear arms was sent to defend them.

Suddenly German resistance collapsed —civilians came out of their cellars and cleared the road blocks away; sheets appeared from upstairs windows. By midday American armour was in the town centre. At 1520 light aircraft from the two armoured divisions were in radio contact and each had spotted the leading troops of the other. Ten minutes later the 1 April link-up was official, although patrols made contact in Lippstadt's eastern suburbs two hours earlier. Bradley's and Montgomery's army groups whose boundary ended at the Rhine had joined up again 150 km (95 miles) farther north-east, enclosing 10,350 square kilometres (4000 square miles) and nearly a third of a million German soldiers.

The great double envelopment had not been achieved without loss: 3rd Armored Division lost 53 tanks and 60 other vehicles and 104th Infantry Division took heavy losses. On First US Army's left flank, 1st Infantry Division also suffered in the stiff fighting. But both divisions set up new records for an infantry advance, the 104th moving 310 km (193 miles) in nine days.

During 2-4 April 1945 the Ruhr's north-east corner was swept clean of German units. From Ninth US Army, 8th Armored Division attacked south-east from Paderborn right into the heart of the Ruhr. Three Ninth Army infantry divisions, struck into the pocket from the north while from the south, First Army attacked with the newly-formed 13th Armored Division and seven infantry divisions.

On 5 April 3rd Corps, in the centre began to attack westwards. Its 9th Infantry Division brushed aside remnants of 9th Panzer Division and gained 6 km (4 miles) while the right-hand 98th Infantry Division advanced 8 km (5 miles). On 6 April the 7th Armored Division took over. On 7 April the sun came out after overcast and rainy days and the Tactical Air Commands' fighter-bombers came out with it, ignoring no targets, not even horse-drawn transport. All ammunition rationing was lifted and the American gunners fired almost round the clock. The artillery supporting a single Corps fired 259,061 rounds during the two-week battle. As the Ruhr Pocket fragmented, the numbers of prisoners rose astronomically. Thousands of Allied POWs were freed.

By midnight on 17 April the Ruhr Pocket was no more. First US Army had closed with the Ninth all along the Ruhr river and the battle for the heart of Germany was over. Ninth Army had suffered 2462 casualties including 341 killed and 121 missing and the First, becaue of strong resistance put up along Model's southern front, had about three times as many casualties.

Model's final decision

On 14 April 1945 Model made his decision. On 17 April he gave his troops the choice of trying to get home, of trying to break out, or of surrendering. Most chose to surrender. It was a mass-surrender that eclipsed Tunisia and Stalingrad, indeed every previous Allied battlefield haul of Axis prisoners, but its significance was to be lost in the evidence of total victory pouring in from all quarters. On 2 May 500,000 German troops capitulated in Italy, and Berlin itself fell. Among the 317,000 Ruhr surrenders were 29 German generals. Not among them was Model, who went into a forest near Dusseldorf and shot himself.

How the great Krupp works at Essen looked after the RAF had paid great interest in the complex, vital to the requirements of German armour and artillery

Hitler said 'We shall not capitulate—no, never. We may be destroyed, but if we are, we shall drag a world with us—a world in flames.'

The Battle of Berlin turned this prophecy into the reality of *Götterdämmerung*. Before 1945, when it was hard to see how it could be done, both the Russians and the Western Allies had repeatedly named Berlin as their goal. But such definitions made little sense unless it was possible to make a proper plan to capture the city. This was not feasible until the beginning of 1945. But once the Wehrmacht had at last recognized that there was nothing left but a strategy of defence the battle for Berlin was on.

Planning the final battle of the war began in the Soviet High Command in October 1944. It was intended to advance from the Vistula to Berlin and beyond in six weeks. The offensive was to start on 20 January. Later the date was brought forward to 12 January. Three army groups or 'fronts' were to attack—1st and 2nd Belorussian commanded respectively by Marshal Georgi K. Zhukov and Konstantin Rokossovski, and 1st Ukrainian under Marshal Ivan S. Koniev—

two and a half million men against fewer than a million Germans. The Russians' material superiority was even greater. When the attack started it had immediate and startling success as the Eastern Front collapsed. By early February the Red Army had reached the river Oder opposite Berlin. They were only 65 km (40 miles) from the city. Here they paused.

'Who is to capture Berlin?'

Why did Stalin not push on after his first brilliant success? He asked his generals: 'Who is to capture Berlin, we or the Allies?'

Zhukov maintained further advance was impossible. Colonel General Vasili I. Chuikov, on the other hand, commanding 8th Guards Army, claimed that the war could have been ended in February.

The result was that the final thrust on Berlin did not start until 16 April. Broadly, Zhukov was to take the city while Koniev would cut off the German Army Group Vistula from Berlin and secure Zhukov's southern flank. Zhukov had no illusions about the problems facing him.

Yet four days after the attack started, his

Far right While the US armies halted on the line of the Elbe, the Russians broke through a threadbare German front to encircle and capture Berlin in two weeks

Far right below A Russian soldier carrying a submachine-gun of 7.62 calibre. He wears the 'Order of the Patriotic War, First Class' on his right breast

Below As Russian shells fall on Berlin, the few remaining German soldiers can only take cover and await the inevitable rape of their great city

artillery opened up on Berlin and on 21 April the leading troops of three armies, 3rd Shock, 2nd Guards Tank and 47th broke into the outskirts of the city. The last phase of the battle had begun. Eleven days later on 2 May, General Helmuth Weidling, Berlin Commandant, surrendered. It was all over. The battle between 16 April and the German capitulation had cost the Red Army a terrible 300,000 casualties.

'How pitiful is their Berlin!' announced Marshal Zhukov after his troops had captured it. It was the Red Army and Allied bombing which had made it so. Yet the courage and perseverance of the Berliners themselves should not be forgotten. The long road to Berlin had cost the Russians 20 million men since that day almost four years earlier when the two great armies had clashed head on. And all of it had been brought about by the man who at the height of the fighting for Berlin conducted the battle which he claimed, would cause the Russians to suffer their bloodiest defeat.

That it was the Russians and not the Americans who reached Berlin first was because of decisions and actions taken during the first two weeks of April 1945. Lieutenant General William H. Simpson's US Ninth Army crossed the Elbe astride Magdeburg on 12 April, and reached Tangemunde—only 80 km (50 miles) from Berlin. The Russians' next offensive was not planned to start for another four days. 16 April, and they were at this time 65 km (40 miles) from Berlin on the Oder. The day before Simpson asked General Omar N. Bradley to let his troops expand the Elbe bridgehead and push on in force for Berlin. That he would have got there seems more or less certain for he had suffered very few casualties and opposite him were only scattered, ill-equipped and untrained formations of General Walther Wenck's Twelfth Army which had no air support at all. Wenck commented: 'If the Americans launch a major attack they'll crack our positions with ease. After all what's to stop them? There's nothing between here and Berlin.' But Eisenhower vetoed the idea.

On the same day Stalin sent a message to the American Ambassador in Moscow to the effect that the Red Army was about to renew the offensive. The main thrust would be on Dresden with a subsidiary one on Berlin. This information was hardly accurate. The main Russian forces were directed at and astride the German capital. Could the Wehrmacht withstand the forthcoming Russian steamroller? Colonel General Gotthard Heinrici in command of Army Group Vistula (still called this although it had long since left the Vistula far away) had

two armies—General Theodor Busse's Ninth Army, directly in the path between the Red Army and Berlin, and General Hasso von Manteuffel's Third Panzer Army which was on the Oder 50 km (30 miles) north-east of the city and was deployed as far north as Stettin. He would be attacked by three Russian Fronts—Rokossovski's aimed at Stettin, Zhukov's at Berlin and Koniev's at Dresden.

It took the Red Army only 10 days from 16 April to surround Berlin. The battle for the Seelow Heights, a critical position, was hard and costly. Despite all their superiority in artillery, the Russian troops came under heavy AT and machine-gun fire which took such a toll of the advancing troops that they were stopped. This caused Stalin to order Koniev to direct his armoured forces on Berlin so that on 17 April two Soviet Fronts were making for the city. This was too much for Busse's Ninth Army, and by 20 April the Germans defending Berlin were overrun.

Before the Russian attack on the Oder position started, Heinrici had explained to Speer that there would be no proper battle for Berlin because the two wings of Army Group Vistula would simply withdraw respectively north and south of the city. But when it was clear to him that Zhukov had broken through, Heinrici did make an attempt to organize the *Volkssturm* battalions to establish some defences to the east of the city. But the *Volkssturm* without transport and with inadequate ammunition could never stop the Red Army.

On 20 April Soviet artillery began to shell

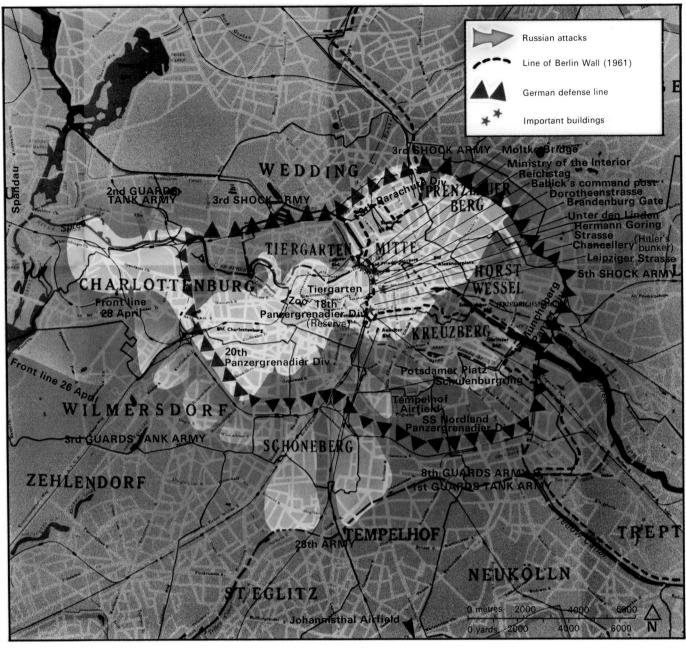

Russian attacks

Line of Berlin Wall (1961)

German defense line

Important buildings

The Russian conquest of Berlin superimposed on a 1944 map compiled by the Office of Strategic Services

Berlin. Next day 2nd Guards Tank, 3rd Shock and 47th Armies—all Zhukov's formations—reached the outskirts of the city. At the same time Koniev was moving forward with 3rd Guards Tank Army. Then with two huge pincer movements, the Russians encircled the German Ninth Army to the south-east of Berlin and Berlin itself, while their spearheads pushed on to the Elbe. By 25 April the Russians had surrounded Berlin and contacted US forces at Torgau. There was only one thing left to do—take Berlin and finish the war in Europe.

Hitler himself had made much of making *Festung Berlin* an impregnable fortress. It was a myth. In March 1945 a 'Basic Order

for the Preparations to Defend the Capital' had been signed and issued, but little had been done to turn Berlin into a proper defensive position. The city was defended more by words than deeds. The battle for Berlin would decide the war, Hitler claimed. So it did, but not in the way he meant. The Basic Order envisaged an outer perimeter about 30 km (20 miles) out, another one 15 km (10 miles) out, a third following the railway serving the suburbs, and a final citadel around the government buildings.

But without troops and weapons, ammunition and supplies or a proper command system to control everything it was but a plan. The battle for the city itself never really developed. It was simply a gigantic mopping-up operation. The Red Army isolated Berlin with overwhelming numbers, slowly crushing the city. It was impossible to fight a full-scale battle there with nearly two million inhabitants, mostly old men or women and children living in shelters. Allied bombing had forced them below ground. In any event the military organization defending the city was a lame skeleton. So-called Panzer divisions had a mere dozen or so tanks and armoured vehicles. After engaging the advancing Russians, they inevitably retreated, leaving the dead and wounded lying in the streets. The fighting itself was done in the midst of civilians who had themselves either been killed by rockets and shells, were cowering in cellars or desperately trying to find further cellars behind the retreating soldiers in order not to fall into Soviet hands. The streets were littered with bodies. Yet in some extraordinary way the spirit of the Berliners survived. They scrawled defiant messages on walls, proclaiming ultimate victory in spite of retreat. It was not the *Gotterdammerung* that Hitler had foreseen. But it had its moments of glory.

Up to 22 April Hitler was still nominally in charge of operations. One day earlier he directed his last battle. First, he gave exact instructions to General Karl Koller, a Luftwaffe officer and Goering's Chief of Staff. When Goering had left the Bunker, Koller stayed. Like so many others he was unable to stand up to Hitler. He would accept the Fuehrer's raving invective and threats with misgivings but without dissent. On this occasion, as so often before, Hitler's orders were given in the greatest detail. He selected precisely which troops were to be brought back into reserve from the northern part of the city in order to launch a counter-attack on the Russians in the southern suburbs. He laid down exactly which ground units of the Luftwaffe were to be employed and in what way. The attack would be an all-out and final attempt to turn the tide. Every man, every gun and every tank would be committed, the Luftwaffe would put every available plane into the skies. All would be staked on a final desperate blow. An SS general *Obergruppenfuehrer* Felix Steiner, would command the operation.

The tactical plan for Steiner's attack was that it would be launched from the Eberswalde into the gap between von Manteuffel's Third Panzer Army and Busse's Ninth Army, so smashing the spearhead of Zhukov's drive on the city. But Army Group Steiner was a figment of Hitler's imagination. It had nothing like the strength required to mount an attack of the sort envisaged. Nonetheless Hitler told Steiner on the telephone to withdraw every man available between Berlin and the Baltic up to Stettin and Hamburg. The order was absurd. Steiner had no communication with any of these troops. Even had he the means of giving orders, there was no transport to move them.

Answerable with his life

The shortage of troops was made up for by an abundance of threats. Commanding officers who did not thrust home would not live to tell the tale. Steiner's written instructions contained a specific promise that he was answerable with his life for the execution of his orders. All was in vain. Hitler's granite willpower was powerless now. Skeleton German battalions could never hold back the fully manned and equipped Russian divisions. The attack never came off. It did not even cross the start-line. German withdrawal in the north simply allowed Russian tanks to stampede through to the centre of Berlin.

Weidling, on the other hand, who became

A Russian artillery piece lobs a shell over ruined buildings in a Berlin street. Nearby a knocked-out German tank typifies the beaten state of the once all-conquering Wehrmacht. Due to Hitler's obstinacy Berlin was all but destroyed but he never lived to see the final horrific hours as the Red Army took its revenge

Above Red Army soldiers advance through the centre of ruined Berlin. The wrecked Reichstag can just be seen through the smoke and dust

Below Caution is shown by the Russian soldiers as they investigate a Berlin subway. Now and again they hit pockets of brave but futile resistance and dealt with it without mercy

Commandant of Berlin on 25 April, knew the city was almost surrounded. That evening on reporting in the Bunker to the Fuehrer and his entourage, he showed them from a sketch map that the ring around the city would soon be finally closed. In fact the ring was already closed. The encirclement involved eight Soviet armies. On the same day, 25 April, Hitler ordered the Wehrmacht to re-establish contact with Berlin by attacking from the north-west, south-east and south—so bringing the battle of Berlin to a 'victorious conclusion'. The only troops Weidling had, would ever have, were some *Volkssturm* battalions, Luftwaffe ground personnel and Hitler Youth units, and the remainder of his own 56 Panzer Corps.

Despite all these difficulties Weidling made a plan which he put to the Fuehrer on 26 April for effecting Hitler's escape from the city. Hitler rejected it. He was not prepared to be caught wandering about somewhere in the woods: 'I stay here to die at the head of my men. But you must continue to defend the city.'

On 23 April Stalin laid down the boundary between Zhukov and Koniev. The *Reichstag* (Parliament Building), where the Soviet flag was to be raised, was given to Zhukov. His soldiers captured the building and ran up the Red Flag at about 1430 on 30 April—an hour before Hitler committed suicide. But German resistance continued in the hands of an SS officer, *Obersturmfuehrer* Babick. His post was not in the *Reichstag* itself but in the cellar of the house on the corner of Dorotheenstrasse and the Hermann Goering Strasse. There he ruled from an air-raid shelter. Against the wall stood an old sofa and in front of it a dining-table on which a map of the centre of Berlin was spread out. Sitting on the sofa was an elderly marine commander and next to him two petty officers. Babick, bending over his map, treated everyone present in the dim candle-lit room to great pearls of military wisdom.

He was hoping for reinforcements. From somewhere or another, marines had come to Berlin on the night of 28 April.

Ranks in the *Reichstag* got thinner and thinner and by the night of 30 April, no more than 40 to 50 people, soldiers and civilians, were left in the cellar. This remnant was now busy looking for the safest possible hiding-places. At dawn on 1 May, it was learned that the Fuehrer had fallen in the battle for the *Reich* capital, his wife at his side. Joseph Goebbels and his family had gone the same way.

The only thing still to be done was to negotiate with the Russians in order to surrender what was left of the city. By this time all that was left in German hands were the Government buildings, part of the adjoining *Tiergarten* and the area between the Zoo and the Havel river. Hitler had forbidden Weidling to capitulate but he had authorized a break-out. After Hitler's death Martin Bormann, the Deputy Fuehrer, had sent a telegram to Admiral Karl Donitz in Plon, appointing him as Hitler's successor. Donitz, not realizing that Hitler was dead, replied: 'My Fuehrer! My loyalty to you will be unconditional. I shall do everything possible to relieve you in Berlin. If fate nevertheless compels me to rule the *Reich* as your appointed successor, I shall continue this war to an end, worthy of the unique, heroic struggle of the German people.' But Goebbels and Bormann were trying above all to put an end to the pointless bloodshed. They therefore made contact with the Russians who agreed to receive a German representative.

This was Lieutenant General Hans Krebs, Chief of the General Staff, who spoke Russian and had been in Moscow as Military Attache. He met General Chuikov, Commander of the 8th Guards Tank Army, at Schulenburgring near Tempelhof Airport, at 0400 on the morning of 1 May. He had been authorized to negotiate only a truce or armistice, but the Russians, despite suspicions that the Western Allies were contemplating a separate peace with the German armies in the West, refused to consider anything except unconditional surrender. Thus Krebs failed and he committed suicide after returning to the Bunker. Next Weidling tried to negotiate. On the following morning he crossed the line dividing the two armies and surrendered the Berlin garrison with its 70,000 troops. The battle for Berlin was over. The question now was how would the Russians behave?

Rape, looting, burning and murder became commonplace. Hitler's very last War Directive of 15 April had made it clear what fate threatened a defeated Germany: 'While the old men and children will be murdered, the women and girls will be reduced to barrack-room whores.' Even at the end Hitler's reliance on propaganda and foresight did not desert him. But better things were on the way for Berlin. The Red Army positioned more disciplined regiments there; American troops reached the city on 1 July; the British arrived next day.

It was the end of the war in Europe.

Beneath the Russian soldiers raising the Red Flag atop the shattered Reichstag lies Berlin, nothing but rubble and flames. The building was the scene of some of Adolf Hitler's most bombastic statements, all of which came to nothing at the end of the war in Europe